BOOTS ON
THE GROUND
AMERICA'S WAR IN VIETNAM

VIKING
An imprint of Penguin Random House LLC
375 Hudson Street
New York, New York 10014

First published in the United States of America by Viking,
an imprint of Penguin Random House LLC, 2018

LIBRARY OF CONGRESS CATALOGING-IN-PUBLICATION DATA
Names: Partridge, Elizabeth, author.
Title: Boots on the ground : America's war in Vietnam /
Elizabeth Partridge.
Other titles: America's war in Vietnam
Description: New York : Viking,
published by Penguin Group, [2018] |
Audience: Grades 7–8. | Audience: Ages 12 and up. |
Identifiers: LCCN 2017013227 (print) | LCCN 2017015217
(ebook) | ISBN 9780425291788 (ebook) |
ISBN 9780670785063 (hardcover) |
ISBN 9780142423752 (trade pbk.)
Subjects: LCSH: Vietnam War, 1961–1975—
United States—Juvenile literature. |
Vietnam War, 1961–1975—Biography—Juvenile literature.
Classification: LCC DS558 (ebook) | LCC DS558 .P38 2018
(print) | DDC
959.704/3373—dc23
LC record available at https://lccn.loc.gov/2017013227

Manufactured in Malaysia   Set in IM Fell Pro
JACKET AND BOOK DESIGN BY JIM HOOVER

10   9   8   7   6   5   4   3   2   1

A NOTE ABOUT LANGUAGE

There are offensive words in some quoted material in this
book, particularly racial slurs that were meant to denigrate
and be hurtful. Though these derogatory words are no less
offensive today, I have not censored them. They are important
for understanding the Vietnam War, its era, and the intense
memories and feelings of several of my interviewees.

For Tom Ratcliff

MAP *of* SOUTHEAST ASIA DURING THE VIETNAM WAR

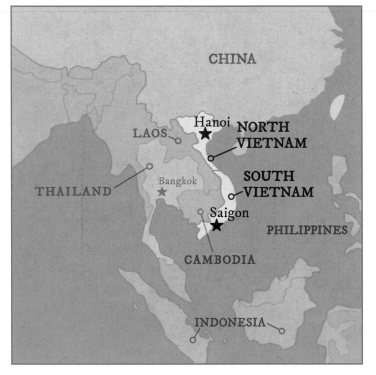

DETAIL of VIETNAM: 1954–1975

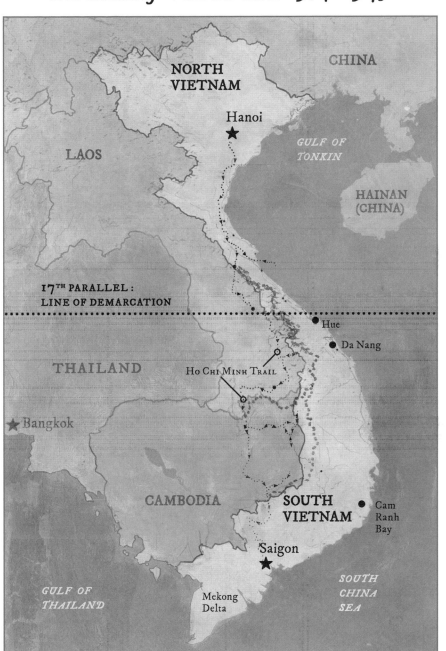

CONTENTS

The author, Elizabeth Partridge, and her boyfriend, Warren Franklin, 1968.

PROLOGUE
November 1968

AS SOON AS the hitchhiker climbed into the backseat next to me, I was sorry we had picked him up. Standing by the road in a coat and hat, he'd looked like one of us—a teenager heading out of town Friday night, away from parents and school. But inches away, he felt tense and vigilant. He reminded me of a cougar, muscles taut, ready to spring.

John and Warren, in front, laughed over a joke as we sped onto the freeway. We were headed for John's family cabin in the mountains, and we could get the hitchhiker halfway to Reno, Nevada, where he was headed. He adjusted the heavy duffel bag on his lap and pulled off his knit hat. His hair was short. Military short.

"Where're you coming from?" asked John, glancing in the rearview mirror. Warren turned around, took one startled look at the hitchhiker's short hair, and swung back.

"Nam," the hitchhiker said. He looked at us warily, taking in our love beads, and John's and Warren's long hair.

"Nam?" asked John.

There was a long pause. "I'm a Green Beret," the hitchhiker finally said. "Been in Vietnam a year."

Vietnam. It was like a concussion grenade smashed against the windshield and ricocheted back through the car. *The Vietnam War.* It was stalking us all. We were high-school seniors, and the clock was ticking: once out of high school all American males faced two years of compulsory military service. When they turned eighteen, men had to register with the Selective Service System, the agency responsible for implementing a draft. With thousands of soldiers being sent to Vietnam, there were not enough volunteers for the military to meet troop needs. We watched anxiously as people we knew were drafted into the army. It didn't matter whether they volunteered or were drafted, if they were ordered to Vietnam, they would be there for twelve months.

Three years earlier, President Lyndon B. Johnson had sent troops to aid the South Vietnamese government in its fight against the Communist North Vietnamese. Every night on the news, we watched footage of battles. The sound of machine-gun fire and exploding bombs reverberated off our living-room walls. Villagers ran from combat clutching small children as news anchors reported ever-growing numbers of Americans killed in action. It was horrible to watch, but impossible not to.

Warren, John, and I went to Berkeley High School, in California. We were in the West Coast epicenter of the military as they shipped men and equipment across the Pacific to Vietnam. The San Francisco Bay Area was a constant flash point for demonstrations and marches against the war. I was a dreamy, bookish girl, not inclined to politics and protest. But the war made me feel desperate, and I wanted it to end. All I could do was join the street protests, add my body to the crowd.

We didn't mix, those of us against the war and the guys who came back from Vietnam. And now I was sitting next to someone just out of Vietnam, fresh from his job to kill or be killed. I pulled away from him, moved closer to my window. What had he seen in Vietnam? What had he done?

It was a long, awkward drive. We didn't ask him any questions, and he volunteered nothing.

When we finally arrived at the cabin, it was past midnight, with a heavy, wet snow falling. We couldn't leave him by the side of the road, and invited him in for the night. He sat in a corner of the kitchen as we made a late meal. He was perfectly still except his eyes, which flicked from the door to the dark windows, to our faces and back to the door. I couldn't shake the feeling that if some perceived danger set him off, he was ready to spring.

He slept on the living-room floor rolled in a blanket. When we woke up in the morning, he was gone.

A National Guard helicopter sprays tear gas on protestors at the University of California, Berkeley, 1969.

AFTER GRADUATION, JOHN enrolled in college, which deferred his military service. Warren was ordered by the Selective Service, the agency in charge of the draft, to report for his physical. He was given a medical deferment for the braces he wore on his teeth, and told to report back in a year. I started college at nearby UC Berkeley, where my life was a mixture of antiwar rallies and marches and beginning French and rhetoric classes. Men were still being drafted, and Americans and Vietnamese were dying. Why couldn't we—or wouldn't we—get out of Vietnam?

A lot of protestors wanted to know the same thing. Peaceful gatherings became violent as frustrated demonstrators threw rocks and bottles, even started fires. I hated being in the middle of the unruly, angry crowds. Policemen and the National Guard retaliated with tear gas, helicopters, and bullets. How had we come to this, where violence was used to protest violence?

I went to more classes and fewer protests, until I steered clear of demonstrations completely. But conflict was unavoidable. As I came out of class one day, a helicopter

swept over campus and released a wide arc of tear gas meant for a nearby rally. I ran blindly back into the building, coughing and choking, my lungs and eyes on fire.

Our country had irrevocably split in two: those for the war, and those against.

In April 1975, the North Vietnamese Communists swept down through South Vietnam, heading for the capital, Saigon. On April 23, President Gerald R. Ford announced the war was finished as far as America was concerned. Five days later, as North Vietnamese troops encircled Saigon, Ford ordered the evacuation of all United States citizens from Vietnam. Helicopters plucked the last desperate Americans from the roof of the embassy.

More than a million Americans had served in combat or in at-risk support teams in Vietnam. There had been no parades, no celebrations to welcome anyone home. Those who'd served in Vietnam kept their heads down and did their best to readjust privately to civilian life. Like most Americans whose lives were not directly touched by the war, I put it behind me and went on with my life. I was just relieved the fighting was over.

National Guardsmen, called out by the governor to quell demonstrations, surround a Vietnam War protester during the People's Park Riot in Berkeley, California, 1969. The Guardsmen herded protesters into a parking lot with bayonets.

A FEW YEARS ago, I visited Washington, DC. Our complicated military involvement in the Middle East made me think once again about the dark, divisive days of the Vietnam War. I walked over to the Vietnam Veterans Memorial, "the Wall," near the Lincoln Memorial. Late-afternoon sunlight slanted through the trees. It was chilly, and few people were in the park. The memorial emerged out of the grass, then as I walked alongside, it rose higher, and higher still. 57,939 American names were inscribed on it in 1982 when it was dedicated, arranged by casualty date—the day the person was killed, or sustained wounds that led to death. I ran my fingers over the tiny, chiseled letters. So many dead. Buddies who'd died together now clustered together forever in the granite.

57,939 is an abstract number, but name after name under my fingertips was not. How *had* this happened, that we'd been drawn deeper and deeper into the war, at such great cost? So many lives lost, both Americans and Vietnamese.

A young man with an open face came up to me. "Could you do me a favor?" he asked. He waved his cell phone apologetically. "My grandmother asked me to take a photograph of my grandfather's name," he said. "And my battery's dead."

I used my phone to take a picture of him pointing to his grandfather's name, Galen E. Haynie, and texted it to him. He thanked me, glad to have a picture for his grandmother, and loped off.

Long ago, back in 1969, Galen E. Haynie had died in Vietnam. He'd left a widow at home with a child to raise. Later, there was a cheerful grandson. The war continued to reverberate through our country, through these dead.

I put both my hands flat on the granite. It was still warm, a gentle radiance of the day's earlier sunlight. Tears filled my eyes, surprising me. How could I be crying for people I'd never known?

In a sudden flash, I remembered the hitchhiking Green Beret. He must have had friends whose names were chiseled into the granite. Had he come here to pay his respects, to remember?

Who *were* they, all these Americans who left the United States—volunteers and

Galen E. Haynie's grandson points out his grandfather's name on the Vietnam Veterans Memorial, Panel 18W, Row 129, 2014.

draftees—to fight in a war far away? Where were the men who'd come back, who'd laughed and eaten and fought alongside their buddies in Vietnam, mourned them in death? Where were the women who'd cared for the injured and dying?

I set out to find a few of these veterans. I wanted to hear their stories, understand what their time in Vietnam had been like.

Overleaf: *Vietnam Veterans Memorial, Washington, DC, 2014.*

Mike Horan with his fifty-pound field transport pack on the Okinawa military base in Japan, 1962. His

VIETNAM: MILITARY ADVISOR

MIKE HORAN
IN COUNTRY MAY 1962–JUNE 1963

"They put a rope around my neck, tied my hands, and they dragged me around wherever they went. I was basically a running prisoner. They were some really nasty guys. I thought that I probably would be tortured. I was sure I was going to get killed."

EVER SINCE HE was about five years old, Mike Horan had been in the foster care system, moved from one family to another. At every new school, there were always boys who wanted to test him out, see how tough he was. They'd surround him in a corner of the yard, taunting, fists striking. After getting beat up a few times, he'd had enough. *If you're going to come and fight*, he thought, *then we're going to fight*. He started hitting back, hard. He'd learned his lesson: nobody was going to stick up for him, so he'd better take care of himself.

He did have one good foster placement, with the Mallon family in Indiana. The Mallons' son, Jimmy, was just one year younger than Horan. They spent hours building model airplanes, talking and dreaming about cars, and playing on the school's softball team. Even after Horan was pulled from the Mallons at the end of the school year and put in a new foster home, he and Jimmy stayed in touch. The Mallons were the closest he had to family.

Horan (left) and his friend Jimmy Mallon, who was later killed in Vietnam and is honored on the Wall on Panel 28E, Row 61, 1953.

By eleventh grade, after more than a dozen schools, Horan was barely passing his classes. He worried about how he was going to support himself after high school. It looked like only dead-end jobs out there for someone like him, working in a gas station or on the assembly line at a nearby tire factory. Horan decided to join the military. Right after he graduated, he signed up for four years with the Marines.

Basic training was a shock. "Boot camp was pretty tough," Horan said. "A lot of physical effort, calisthenics, and endurance exercises. A lot of mental intimidation, a lot of inspections." Sometimes new recruits were punished for something they didn't do well enough, or someone in their platoon didn't do well enough: cleaning their boots, pitching a tent, performing in drill competitions. "You were expected to do what you were told," Horan said, "and don't think about it—just do it." He found out fast that it was a bad idea to argue with his superiors, even when he was sure he was right. "They would hate my guts," Horan said, "so they would just give me the worst duty." Horan realized he had to do what he was told, when he was told, and keep his mouth shut.

In May 1962, Horan was sent to the American base in Okinawa, Japan, and assigned to Charlie Company, 3rd Reconnaissance Battalion. Like the other Marines, Horan had only a rough idea of why his battalion was there. After World War II, a "cold war" had begun between the democratic United States and the Communist Soviet Union. The two countries struggled for supremacy using political maneuvering, stockpiling weapons, and fighting "proxy" wars in other, smaller countries where they didn't directly engage each other. American leaders fervently believed in the "domino theory": if one country became Communist, the country next to it would fall to Communism, then the next, like a row of dominoes, rapidly knocking each other over. The fear was that in the end, even the United States would be overrun by Communists.

Vietnam, not far from Japan, was seen as an important line in the sand for holding back Communism. In 1954, the country had been divided in two at the 17th parallel. North Vietnam, led by president Ho Chi Minh, was Communist, and South Vietnam, under president Ngo Dinh Diem, was democratic. Ho Chi Minh was intent on reuniting his country under Communism. The American president, John F. Kennedy, felt it was critical to provide military and economic aid to South Vietnam so it would remain democratic.

From the American base in Japan, Horan and other members of the 3rd Recon were deployed into Saigon, the capital of South Vietnam. He was now "in country," military slang for serving in Vietnam. The Marines were officially there as military advisors to train the Army of the Republic of Vietnam (ARVN), the ground forces of South Vietnam. American helicopters would fly ARVN troops into the field, and accompany them on combat missions.

South Vietnamese Army troops in combat operations against the Communist Viet Cong guerillas, 1961.

Because the terrain was so unfamiliar to the Americans, a large part of their time was spent training for jungle combat. "We were all busy hiking and camping in the jungle," Horan said, "learning how things got done, how to set up patrols, how to set up ambushes, how to take the fight to the enemy.

"It was exciting on one hand, but it was pretty scary on the other," said Horan. Just being in the jungle was miserable. The air was stifling hot and humid. Rain fell in drenching downpours. "If you went into a river or a lake, you were probably going to get leeches on you," Horan said. "There were snakes all over the place, and I couldn't stand snakes."

Horan was horrified when he realized the jungle trails were rigged with "punji" traps. The Communists dug deep holes in the trail, shoved razor-sharp bamboo spikes

Constructing a punji trap, undated photo.

into the hole with the points up, and then covered everything with branches and leaves. Some of Horan's buddies had brand-new boots with a metal plate in the sole for protection, but Horan didn't. The treacherous footing terrified him. One misstep, and he could fall into a hole, the sharp spikes tearing through his boot sole into his foot. Rumors flew that the spikes were coated with human feces. Wounds festered and got infected at lightning speed in the damp heat.

Despite the life-and-death stakes, the Marines were eager to engage the enemy. "Most guys in our unit outfit wanted to get into combat," Horan said. "They wanted to do what they had been trained to do." So did Horan.

At unexpected times, Horan would be ordered to grab his gear and load into a waiting helicopter with five or six other Marines. They would be set down in the jungle, sometimes with ARVN troops, and told to try to locate the enemy. They were often searching for small bands of Viet Cong (VC), South Vietnamese farmers allied with the North Vietnamese cause. The VC operated as guerrilla fighters in clandestine, deadly efficient groups. Since they wore no uniforms, it was impossible to tell friend from foe. "Rice farmers by day, VC by night" became the wary watchword of the Marines.

Out in the jungle on patrol, fear of a sudden assault kept Horan's nerves on edge. Before the Marines even spotted anyone, shooting could suddenly erupt from the dense foliage of the jungle. They would have to quickly organize into a defensive perimeter. But just as fast as the attack had started, it would stop, and the VC would be gone. Under fire, officers quickly earned Horan's respect as they made rapid, life-saving decisions. "I would have followed them to hell if there was a firefight going on," he said.

Fortunately for the unseasoned Marines, attacks were rare. "Most of the time, nothing would happen," said Horan. "The VC would figure out that we were there, and they didn't want to mess with us." Massively outgunned, the Communists made sure they fought when and where they had an advantage, then disappeared.

In early 1963, Horan was selected to be part of a five-man American team working on the Strategic Hamlet Program. Initiated in the United States, the program was intended to stop the Viet Cong who infiltrated farming villages at night and forced villagers to side with the Communists. By 1963, the South Vietnamese government had relocated more than five million farmers to heavily fortified villages.

"We would go around to these villages and set up perimeters of defense," Horan explained. His team would spend several days with the men in the village, inside the fence made of enormous bamboo stakes or barbed wire. They'd hand out rifles and pistols and show the men how to defend themselves from a Viet Cong attack.

Horan's team was sent to one of the new fortified villages north of Saigon, reached by a narrow, pothole-filled dirt road, barely passable in their open jeep. Horan taught the villagers how to take the rifles apart, clean, load, and fire them. To his surprise, the villagers were nervous about the guns. He needed to show them over and over again how to handle the weapons.

The team stayed in the village for four days, eating meals prepared by the villagers. Horan liked the soups and the rice, but he didn't dare try the other food they served, with cooked snakes, frog legs, and other animals hunted from the jungle. He supplemented his soup and rice with canned C rations he'd brought with him: familiar American food like beans and franks, even if he had to eat it cold from the can. At night, Horan and the other men rolled out their poncho liners—thin, quilted nylon blankets that provided a little warmth—and slept on the packed dirt floor of a hut. By the time they left, Horan was confident the men knew how to use the guns to defend themselves.

Three weeks later, the team returned to the village with an assignment from their superiors: file a report detailing the villagers' improvement in self-defense. When the Americans arrived, the villagers seemed glad to see them, welcoming them and offering tea and food. But the team couldn't find any of the men they'd talked to before. "Where are the guns?" Horan asked. "Where's the

More than eight million villagers were forcibly removed from their ancestral homes in a joint US and South Vietnam program. As shown here, they were required to fortify their new strategic hamlets, 1962. Villagers also had to pay for items like bamboo, concrete fence posts, and barbed wire. The obligatory labor meant less time to cultivate their own fields.

ammo?" Smiling, shrugging, the villagers shook their heads apologetically. It slowly dawned on the Americans that either the Viet Cong had come and stolen it all, or they'd just been directly training and arming the Viet Cong. "Basically, they tricked us," Horan admitted. It was a humiliating realization.

Angry and feeling duped, the team piled into the jeep for the ride home. Their attempt to aid South Vietnam was more than a failure: they had actually *helped* arm the enemy. Eager to leave, they roared out of the village on the narrow dirt road. They hadn't gone far when the jeep hit a land mine. There was a deafening blast, and the jeep flew up into the air.

The explosion threw Horan into a ditch. He lay there, stunned, not able to hear anything. After a couple of minutes, he realized there was a firefight going on around him. Suddenly he was rushed from behind. Several guerrillas roughly pulled him out of the ditch. He looked wildly around for the other Americans, but didn't see them anywhere. The guerrillas tied a rope around his neck, bound his hands, and dragged him with them as they ran into the jungle. He had no idea why they took him, or where they were going. Where were the other Americans? Had any others been taken prisoner, or had they all been killed?

He had four captors. They wore no uniforms, so Horan knew they weren't regular North Vietnamese Army (NVA) troops. They were either farmers who were secretly Viet Cong, or they were members of one of the small mountain tribes fighting alongside the Communists. Whoever they were, they were rough, hardened men who looked like they'd been living in the jungle for a long time, eating what they could scrounge, sleeping on the ground. They were filthy, and smelled disgusting to Horan.

For the next few days, the guerrillas stuck to narrow jungle footpaths, moving at a steady jog to avoid any of the American or South Vietnamese patrols in the area. Horan, badly bruised and terrified, his finger sliced open from when he'd been thrown from the jeep, struggled to keep up with the punishing pace they set. "They would exhaust me every time," he said. Gulping for air, his leg muscles shaking with fatigue, he'd finally stumble and fall to the ground. The guerrillas would stand over him, berating and humiliating him in Vietnamese. They'd kick him a few times to get him back on his feet, then they'd yank on his neck rope and start running again.

These Viet Cong prisoners are ready to be transported by the ARVN, 1964. Both North and South Vietnam interrogated prisoners in an attempt to gain military information.

Several times a day, the guerrillas would stop to rest, and dip into a dirty cloth bag holding cooked rice mixed with some kind of fish or meat. Sometimes Horan would be given a small handful. He no longer had the luxury of caring what he ate. He wolfed it down. Sometimes they didn't offer him any, and he could only watch as they ate, his stomach twisting with hunger. After everyone drank at a stream, they were up and moving again.

Horan had no idea why they wanted him, but they were clearly headed somewhere. He figured they were going to turn him over to someone with more authority. "I was petrified," he said. Deeply hidden inside the jungle were a scattering of small prisons, often just bamboo cages that held one man, forced to sit or crouch. Maybe they were taking him to one of those.

Escape was impossible. He was always with his captors, held by the rope around his neck. His hands were bound tightly together. Even if he got a chance to run, he had no food, no compass, and no idea where he was. The jungle foliage was so thick, he could barely even see the sun. And after his experience being tricked in the fortified village, he doubted any Vietnamese would help him. "I was just trying to stay alive," said Horan, "do what I had to do." He kept putting one foot in front of the other. For that moment, for that one step, he was still alive.

The guerrillas tried to get information out of him, yanking on his rope and firing rapid questions at him in Vietnamese or a few words of broken English. He didn't speak any Vietnamese, but he guessed the gist of what they were asking. It was futile to say he was just a low-ranking soldier following orders. Communication was impossible.

After several days, one of the guerrillas began questioning him again on a rest break. The man put his face close to Horan's and began screaming angry questions at him. Suddenly the guerrilla forced Horan's head back and held a knife against his throat.

Time stopped. The man's contorted face was inches from Horan's, his breath fetid. The sharp blade of the knife pressed into Horan's skin. The next few seconds unfolded in his mind: he was going to get his throat slit, and be left to bleed to death by the side of the trail.

The one thing he could do now was die with dignity. "I didn't yell, or scream, or beg," Horan said. It took all his willpower to hold absolutely still, his heart pounding in his ears. "I just waited." He refused to give them the satisfaction of seeing him grovel.

The man abruptly shoved Horan face-first into the dirt and started laughing uproariously, joined by the others. "Here I was on the ground," Horan said, "glad that I was alive, but being made fun of." Where would this all end? Would he just be tortured and humiliated until he was finally killed?

A day later, sitting on the edge of a field taking a break, the guerrillas suddenly became agitated. They jumped to their feet in alarm, speaking rapidly to one another, then ran off into the jungle. What was going on? Why had they abruptly left him, after bringing him this far? He stood, desperately straining his eyes and ears for information.

At first, he didn't hear or see anything. Moments later, a Marine appeared on the far side of the field. Another joined him, and soon Horan was looking at a whole platoon doing a search of the area. An officer spotted him and rapidly walked over. At first he seemed to think Horan, still in his uniform, was part of his platoon. "What the hell are you doing here?" the officer barked.

Horan recited his name, service number, and unit. He was filthy, thirsty, hungry, and exhausted. But he'd never been so elated in his life. He was alive. He was safe.

The Marines cut the rope from his neck, and gave him water and all the C rations he could eat. They didn't question him about what had happened while he was a prisoner, just had him wait until someone came to drive him back to his unit.

Horan's commanding officer asked him to account for his absence: where had he been the last few days? Horan went over the failure of the strategic hamlet, the land mine, and being taken prisoner. He didn't know who had captured him, or why. The officer didn't seem to care that he'd been missing, and said nothing about what had happened to the other men in the jeep. "Go pick up your regular duties," the officer said to Horan. "Get out of here."

"Yes, sir," replied Horan. He had his finger sewn up and went back to his unit.

Horan was flat-out glad to be alive, and relieved to be back in the safety and relative comfort of the Marine Corps. But the officer's lack of concern cut him to the quick. His commanding officer didn't even bother to note Horan's experience in his service record. After what Horan had been through, it was demoralizing. It felt typical of the dismissive behavior some officers with college degrees had toward enlisted men like him. "You learn in the Marine Corp," Horan said, "right from day one, that the officers have the college degrees and they're in charge, and the enlisted have high school diplomas. And they do the grunt work. And so you realize really how much discrimination there is, based just on education."

Horan finished his tour of duty in Vietnam and returned to the States with a plan. "My first goal—my overriding goal—was to become an educated person," he said. He was determined to go to college.

President John F. Kennedy at his desk in the Oval Office, 1962.

AMERICA:
PRESIDENT AND COMMANDER IN CHIEF

JOHN F. KENNEDY
NOVEMBER 1963

"This is another type of war, new in its intensity, ancient in its origin—war by guerrillas, subversives, insurgents, assassins, war by ambush instead of by combat; by infiltration, instead of aggression, seeking victory by eroding and exhausting the enemy instead of engaging him."

MONDAY, NOVEMBER 4, 1963. President John F. Kennedy sat at his desk in the Oval Office, a heavy weight on his mind. Two days earlier, the president of South Vietnam, Ngo Dinh Diem, and his brother Ngo Dinh Nhu had been overthrown in a violent coup by their own generals.

Kennedy reached for the Dictaphone sitting on the table behind him to record his private thoughts. He reflected on his role—a tragically important role—in the coup. "Over the weekend the coup in Saigon took place," he said. He'd held many divisive meetings with his advisors about the political and military situation in Vietnam. The coup "culminated three months of conversation about a coup, conversation which divided the government here and in Saigon," Kennedy said into the microphone. "I feel that we must bear a good deal of responsibility for it, beginning with our cable of early August in which we suggested the coup."

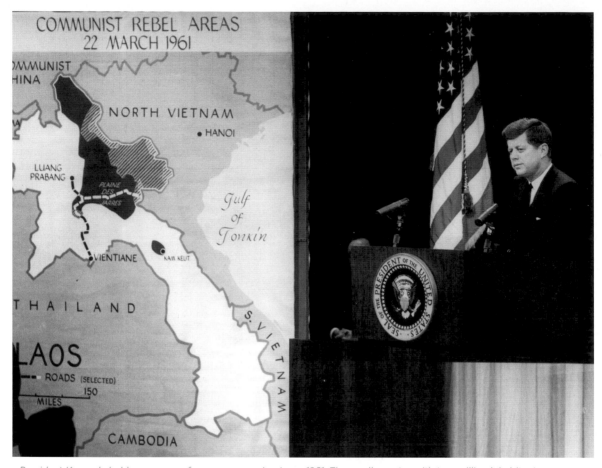

President Kennedy holds a news conference concerning Laos, 1961. The small country with two million inhabitants was, like Vietnam, considered an important place to halt Communist domination of Southeast Asia.

It was a brutally honest admission, spoken aloud in the Oval Office. Several months earlier, Kennedy had given the green light to the top secret Cable 243, sent by the US State Department to the American ambassador stationed in Saigon, South Vietnam.

Initially, Kennedy had enthusiastically supported President Diem. In 1961, when Kennedy had taken office, there were seven hundred American military advisors in Vietnam. He had quickly increased their numbers, until now there were 16,000. But Diem's government had become increasingly corrupt and repressive. His chief advisor, his younger brother Nhu, was especially brutal, and had just masterminded an inhumane crackdown on the country's Buddhists.

Though cloaked in diplomatic language, Cable 243's meaning had been clear to the American ambassador. The United States demanded Diem remove his brother from power, and laid out the consequences if he did not. "If, in spite of all your efforts," the cable to the ambassador read, "Diem remains obdurate and refuses, then we must face the possibility that Diem himself cannot be preserved." Diem had no intention of distancing himself from his brother. In Vietnam, the ambassador called a meeting to discuss a clandestine coup. To ensure American involvement would not be evident, he turned it over to the Central Intelligence Agency (CIA), an organization that gathers information around the world regarding American national security. The CIA operated covertly in Vietnam, as it did in many countries, and let

Vice President Lyndon B. Johnson (left) meets with President Kennedy in the Oval Office two months before Kennedy's assassination, 1963.

the Vietnamese generals know the Americans would turn a blind eye to their plans.

Quietly implementing policies about South Vietnam was nothing new for the president. Besides increasing advisors, he had authorized the spraying of highly toxic Agent Orange and other defoliants to destroy enemy cover in the jungle, as well as rice crops in areas controlled by the Viet Cong.

By the end of October, word reached the White House that the coup appeared imminent. Another series of tense, last-minute meetings took place with the president and his advisors. Weighing the conflicting opinions, it was up to Kennedy to make a critical choice: stand by Cable 243, or retract it. At one meeting, Kennedy scrawled "coup" four times on a sheet of paper.

He decided to let the cable stand.

It was a grisly murder. On November 2, President Diem and his brother Nhu were shot to death and Diem was repeatedly stabbed in a coup led by Vietnamese generals. Despite the hard-line choice Kennedy had made, he found Diem's death shocking. "The way he was killed made it particularly abhorrent," Kennedy admitted on his Dictaphone recording.

The coup was a huge, fateful step into the quicksand that Vietnam was rapidly becoming for the United States. Though reporters had no idea of the president's complicity with the Vietnamese generals, they were eager to know how the coup would affect American involvement in Vietnam. Kennedy assured the press that his goal was "to bring Americans home" and "permit the South Vietnamese to maintain themselves as a free and independent country." He said he planned to pull some of the advisors out of Vietnam by the end of the year. "I don't want the United States to have to put troops there," he said.

It's impossible to know if Kennedy meant it, or if he could have pulled it off. A week later, on November 22, he was assassinated, shot while riding in an open car in Dallas, Texas. Within hours, his vice president, Lyndon B. Johnson, was sworn in as president.

First Lady Jacqueline Kennedy, her children, Caroline and John Junior, and other family members leave the US Capitol Building where the late president lies in state, 1963.

President Johnson used his imposing physical stature and outsized personality to intimidate others, 1965. Known as the "Johnson Treatment," he would bully, flatter, and cajole to get his way.

AMERICA:
PRESIDENT AND COMMANDER IN CHIEF

LYNDON B. JOHNSON
AUGUST 1964–DECEMBER 1965

"We are not about to send American boys 9 or 10,000 miles away from home to do what Asian boys ought to be doing for themselves."

AS VICE PRESIDENT, Johnson had disagreed with Kennedy on the coup against Diem. Now the weight of America's involvement in the whole complicated, messy conflict in Vietnam sat squarely on his shoulders. Throughout the spring, he rarely mentioned Vietnam to reporters or in his speeches. As much as possible, he wanted to keep Vietnam out of the newspapers and off the nightly television news reports. He wanted the nation's attention on his sweeping plans for his Great Society initiatives: a series of economic and social reforms to eliminate poverty and social injustice.

But eight months into his presidency, on August 2, 1964, reports from the US destroyer the *Maddox* moved Vietnam to front-page news. As the *Maddox* had plowed through international waters off the North Vietnamese coast in the Gulf of Tonkin, three North Vietnamese patrol boats had attacked the ship. There'd been an exchange of gunfire, and the destroyer had damaged two of the Vietnamese boats and sunk one.

Johnson had a second American destroyer join the *Maddox* and ordered the ships to continue vigorously patrolling. Two days later, an urgent cable arrived from the captain of the *Maddox*. He was under attack again. It was a dark night, with heavy thunderstorms and low clouds, and the *Maddox* immediately began evasive action, zigzagging through the heavy rain and turbulent seas.

The cables kept coming every few minutes or so, reporting more torpedo attacks and bursts of automatic-weapon fire. Abruptly, the cables stopped. A nerve-racking hour went by with no word from the captain. In the White House, their worst fear was that the ship had been sunk. A nearby US aircraft carrier launched fighter aircraft to patrol the skies.

Finally, a fresh cable arrived from the captain of the *Maddox*: "Review of action makes many reported contacts and torpedoes fired appear doubtful. Freak weather effects on radar and overeager sonarmen may have accounted for many reports." Another cable quickly followed: "It is suspected that sonarman was hearing the ship's own propeller beat."

The US fighter planes dipped below the cloud cover. In the driving rain and flashes of lightning, they saw nothing near the two destroyers: no attacking boats, no silvery wakes of torpedoes rushing though the water toward the ships, no bright orange blasts of gunfire.

The president considered his options with his tense advisors. He listened carefully to his secretary of defense, Robert McNamara. If there had been a second, unprovoked attack, McNamara insisted a response was "absolutely necessary." Was there enough evidence to confirm there had been an attack?

Johnson didn't want to be seen as cowardly or as an indecisive leader. He couldn't risk any accusations that he was soft on Communism. Besides, he was never one to back away from a fight. And once in a fight, Johnson hated to lose. Despite conflicting reports, he decided to order immediate retaliatory air strikes. American planes took off from nearby aircraft carriers and made sixty-four sorties over North Vietnam, bombing their torpedo boat fleet and a major oil depot.

Though he had ordered the bombing, Johnson wasn't absolutely convinced the North Vietnamese had initiated another attack. "For all I know," he confided to his press secretary, "our navy was shooting at whales out there."

But Johnson kept moving with assurance, turning the crisis into an opportunity to

President Johnson (left) and his secretary of defense, Robert McNamara, listen to top aides at a National Security meeting on the rapidly evolving situation in Vietnam, 1965.

gain more authority to make independent decisions in Southeast Asia. He went before Congress to ask for the right to "take all necessary measures" to "prevent further aggression." Johnson's public argument that the *Maddox* had been attacked—not once, but twice—was persuasive. As one senator put it: "Our national honor is at stake. We cannot and we will not shrink from defending it." On August 7, both the House and Senate overwhelmingly approved the Gulf of Tonkin Resolution.

In one swift move, Johnson had worked around a critical part of the US Constitution. The framers of the Constitution, to ensure a balance of powers between the executive and legislative branches, had named the president Commander in Chief of the Army and Navy of the United States, but decreed that only Congress could declare war. With passage of the Gulf of Tonkin Resolution, Johnson now had the right to act in Southeast Asia without first getting an official declaration of war from Congress.

Privately, Johnson joked the resolution was "like grandma's nightshirt—it covered everything." He spoke lightly, but Johnson was brilliant at political maneuvers.

He'd seized the moment. Knowing Americans felt threatened, he'd been confident Congress would pass his bill. Now no one could tie his hands or force him into an uncomfortable compromise. He could bomb, put US forces in Vietnam, and initiate large-scale combat operations, all without consulting Congress.

As North Vietnamese attacks in South Vietnam intensified, Johnson decided to run a continuous bombing campaign over North Vietnam aimed at destroying railroads, bridges, roads, and manufacturing plants. He hoped the bombing would bring the North Vietnamese to the negotiating table. But the North Vietnamese were not fazed. As quickly as bridges and buildings were destroyed, hundreds of men and women with picks and shovels were sent to clear the rubble. Repairing and rebuilding began immediately.

General William Westmoreland, the commanding general of US forces in Vietnam, pointed out that the American air base in Da Nang, near the border between North and South Vietnam, was now vulnerable to attack. Johnson agreed to send two battalions of combat troops to protect the base.

On March 8, 3,500 Marines waded ashore at Da Nang. With "boots on the ground," America's involvement in Vietnam changed radically.

Though advisors had died already in Vietnam, sending in combat troops meant many more Americans would be killed. Johnson couldn't keep the mounting death toll a secret. One month after sending in the Marines, he gave a speech defending his choices:

> Tonight Americans and Asians are dying for a world where each people may choose its own path to change. This is the principle for which our ancestors fought in the valleys of Pennsylvania. It is the principle for which our sons fight tonight in the jungles of Vietnam. . . .
>
> The war is dirty and brutal and difficult. And some four hundred young men, born into an America that is bursting with opportunity and promise, have ended their lives on Vietnam's steaming soil.
>
> Why must we take this painful road? . . .

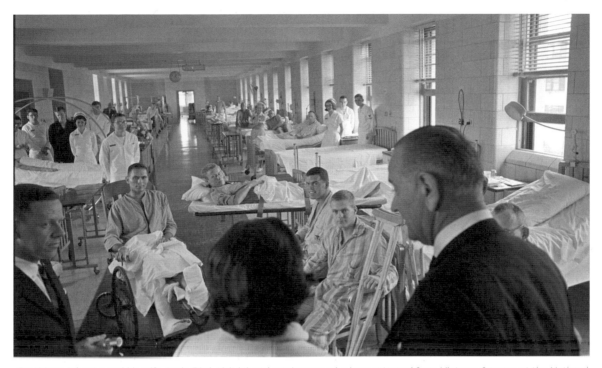

We fight because we must fight if we are to live in a world where every country can shape its own destiny. And only in such a world will our own freedom be finally secure.

His words were measured and thoughtful, his bearing presidential. Lest anyone doubt the importance of what he was doing in Vietnam, he carefully linked American independence and freedom with the "steaming soil" of faraway Vietnam. But off camera, his confidence was paper-thin, and he could be quickly thrown on the defensive. The day before giving the speech, he'd shown an advance copy to a newspaper columnist, hoping to convince him to write a supportive piece the next day. But the columnist had barely finished reading the first page, when Johnson blurted out, "I'm not just going to pull up my pants and run out on Vietnam. You say to negotiate, but there's nobody over there to negotiate with. So the only thing there is to do is to hang on. And that's what I'm going to do."

Just "hanging on" turned out to be impossible as Westmoreland appealed to Johnson for more troops. Johnson agonized. Was he doing the right thing? Were American troops committed to the fight? The more troops he added, the more men would have to be drafted. He worried Americans—especially draftees—just didn't have the same drive as the North Vietnamese.

"They hope they can wear us out," he said. "And I really believe they'll last longer than we do. One of their boys gets down in a rut and he stays there for two days without water, food, or anything and never moves. Waiting to ambush somebody. Now an American, he stays there about twenty minutes and, God damn, he's got to get him a cigarette!"

It wasn't just the soldiers Johnson worried about. A protest movement immediately flared up on campuses across the United States. In Washington, DC, 20,000 people showed up for a protest march.

In early July, Martin Luther King Jr., one of Johnson's biggest allies in the struggle to end racial discrimination, spoke out against the war while addressing civil rights leaders in Virginia. "We won't defeat Communism by bombs and guns and gases. We will do it by making democracy work," said King. "There must be a negotiated settlement even with the Vietcong. The long night of war must be stopped."

King's remarks were carried in *The New York Times*, and he knew Johnson would see the article. In a phone call with the president a few days later, King backpedaled on his comments, trying to soften them. He assured Johnson that what he'd said was "in no way an attempt to engage in a destructive criticism of the policy of the administration. . . . I know the terrible burden and awesome responsibilities and decisions that you have to make are very complicated."

Johnson was quick to blame the North Vietnamese. "I can't stay there and do nothing," he complained to King. "Unless I bomb, they run me out right quick. That's the only pressure we have, and if they'll quit bombing, if they'll quit com-

Five men burn their draft cards in protest against the war, New York City, 1965. The Selective Service required registered men to carry their draft cards at all times. Four of the men went to prison for six months for knowingly destroying or mutilating their cards.

ing in, if they'll quit tearing up our roads and our highways and quit taking over our camps and bombing our planes and destroying them, well, we'll quit the next day if they'll just leave the folks alone, but they won't do it."

At a press conference later in the month, Johnson announced he would send forty-four more combat battalions to Vietnam and would double monthly draft calls to 35,000. By the end of 1965, troop strength in Vietnam had swelled to nearly 200,000 troops.

Gilbert de la O, dressed for a special occasion, in his family's living room, 1962.

VIETNAM:
BOOTS ON THE GROUND

GILBERT DE LA O
IN COUNTRY OCTOBER 1965–SEPTEMBER 1966

"They're coming, man. Get ready."

THE LAST THING on earth Gilbert de la O wanted to do was join the army. But he was caught in a tight spot, running with a rough crowd, fighting, and getting picked up by the cops. He had to figure a way out before he ended up in jail.

De la O was born in Texas, part of a large Mexican American family making a living working in the fields. Every April, his parents would pull him and his siblings out of school. They'd pack the car and drive all the way up to Minnesota to work the crops. While other kids were swimming and playing baseball, de la O was out in the hot sun, weeding, picking beans, and pulling heavy sugar beets out of the ground. When they'd harvested the last crop in October, they'd head back to Texas and school.

Finally de la O's dad landed a full-time job in a meat-packing factory in Saint Paul, Minnesota. The family could settle down and stay in one place. But Anglo kids called de la O and his friends "spics," and "dirty, lazy Mexicans." It stung. "You're not accepted, you're not like the white folks," de la O said. "We became tough guys. . . . You can call us spics and all that, but you know what? We're going to kick your ass, man—and that's what we did."

Even the teachers were against him and the other Mexican American kids. If de la O spoke Spanish in class, he'd be sent to the principal, who'd humiliate him and smack his hand with a ruler.

After graduating from high school, de la O hung out on the street with the West Side Party Boys. That wasn't getting him anything, except to be noticed by the cops. A nearby white gang would drive over to their neighborhood and yell out old insults like "taco benders" and "spic," and things would heat up. That was when de la O decided he better join the military. "I wanted to do my part," he said. "People in my community fought in the army." Besides, he figured being in the military would force people to respect him. *I'm going to go fight for America*, he thought, *so when I come home, they've got to treat me right*. In February 1964, he volunteered for the army.

To his surprise, de la O liked basic training. It was orderly and predictable. He was issued a uniform, equipment, and a rifle. Officers called out his name from their lists. He was always expected to be there and to follow orders exactly. Posted to the Fort Lewis Army Base in Washington, he made friends from all over the country. There was a shared sense of purpose: they were all in it together. He felt included, like he was somebody.

In March 1965, the base buzzed with speculation about the troops being sent to Vietnam. De la O had been at Fort Lewis nearly a year, and he was eager to do some real fighting and prove himself. "I've been here too long, man," he told his company clerk. "I need to get overseas. I need to do something." Several weeks later, his transfer orders came through: he was being sent to Vietnam.

The army gave him a month's leave before sending him overseas, and de la O went home to see his friends and family. "I was really gung-ho," said de la O. "I thought, *Oh, great, I'm going to Vietnam, man*." In the evenings he'd sit with his father and watch the news broadcast on television. Looking at the small firefights and numbers of enemy killed, de la O figured the United States had the upper hand. "I hope we don't win right now," he told his father. "I need to see some action."

On October 1, 1965, de la O was sent to Vietnam and assigned to Charlie Company, 2nd Battalion, 16th Infantry, 1st Infantry Division. After a few days, he was flown out to Camp Ranger, a base camp about twenty miles north of Saigon. When he arrived, Charlie Company was out in the bush, carrying out the new aggressive US strategy of "search and destroy." Troops were ordered to move through a designated

After visiting a wounded friend in the hospital, de la O (left) and his buddy went into Saigon for a beer, 1966.

area, locate VC and NVA troops, and capture or kill them. Success would be measured by body count: the more captured or killed, the closer the Americans and the
South Vietnamese were to victory.

De la O was introduced to his platoon, made up of four squads of seven or eight
guys each. "I was pretty apprehensive, pretty scared," said de la O, "but one of the
things that finally put me to rest was that my squad leader was a Mexican guy, a
Mexican American out of Texas. One of our machine gunners was from Texas also.
So I felt—okay, this is cool."

De la O and the rest of his platoon were sent out in jeeps and trucks to search
nearby villages. The Strategic Hamlet Program initiated by the United States had
failed. VC had infiltrated the strategic hamlets at night and demanded loyalty to the
Communists. Caught in the middle, many villagers sneaked back to their home villages, deserting the strategic hamlets.

When the platoon drove into the villages, they rarely found any men or teenage boys, just women, children, and the elderly. The houses were searched, and everyone in the village rounded up. The squad might be ordered to set the thatched huts on fire, destroying them. They also made sure the villagers couldn't supply the Viet Cong with food. "We killed all the animals that were there," de la O said, "the chickens, the water buffalo, the pigs. We did them all up." Villagers were left homeless, without the animals they depended on for farming, income, and food.

Other days, de la O's platoon was flown into the jungle by helicopter and ordered to find and kill enemy troops. "You go out every day," said de la O. "You were on assignment. You are out there looking for Chuckie—the VC." "Chuckie" was a derisive term coined by infantrymen, using the army's spelling alphabet where a word is assigned to each letter of the alphabet. "VC" became "Victor Charlie," further diminished to "Chuck" or "Chuckie."

The platoon would walk single file through triple-canopy jungle, slashing with machetes when it got dense, hunting for the enemy. The first few times de la O saw a suspected Viet Cong shot, it upset him. But then he'd remind himself what he'd learned in boot camp: *The Vietnamese people don't value life, so to kill them is no biggie.*

An army private shoulders his recoilless rifle as American troops leave the village of Mỹ Tho after setting buildings on fire, 1968.

At the end of the day, when they were told to make camp, de la O was paired up with another guy to dig a foxhole wide enough to sleep in and deep enough to protect them in case of a firefight. "The rain would come, and it would be like buckets falling on top of you," de la O said. "Oh my God, it rained and rained and rained. It was just miserable."

After a meal of C rations, they'd turn in, still wearing their combat clothes and boots. "You do that for a couple weeks and you get dank," said de la O. "It gets to you after a while."

The long, dangerous night, when the Viet Cong were most active, was divided into two-hour shifts. De la O would be awake for two hours, straining his ears, alert for any sounds of someone creeping toward them—a snapped twig, the sound of fabric brushing against a plant. After watch, he'd try to sleep for two hours, then it was time to be back on watch. In the morning, they'd bury their C ration cans and other garbage, and head out for another day of working their way through the jungle.

De la O was always relieved to be back in camp, where there were tents and hot food, and nobody shooting at him. "You're able to relax back there, you get drunk, you do whatever you can," said de la O. But relief would quickly turn to an edgy, nervous kind of boredom, knowing orders would come down soon: maybe a few days, maybe a few weeks. "You wait until the next operation," de la O said, "and then you go out again."

On December 14, word came that another company was pinned down by enemy fire, and de la O and his platoon were ordered to go help. De la O grabbed his gear and loaded into the back of a truck heading for the airstrip to be lifted off by helicopter. As they drove, a grenade suddenly flew toward them and exploded right in the truck. The blast threw de la O to the ground. After the attackers were subdued, he was rushed to the hospital.

De la O's arm, hip, and scalp were filled with shrapnel. A few days later, there was a special ceremony for de la O and the other men who had been injured. They were pinned with Purple Heart medals for their wounds received in action. De la O was proud to be getting a Purple Heart. It was a badge of courage. But he knew he was lucky to have only shrapnel wounds.

A farmer smiles nervously at approaching American troops, one with his weapon at the ready, 1967. There was a rumor among the Americans that Vietnamese wearing black clothing were Viet Cong, and those that wore white were loyal to South Vietnam. Fear and suspicion ran high on both sides.

Within a few weeks, de la O had recovered and was assigned to carry the radio for his commander. In early April 1966, Charlie Company, along with Alpha and Bravo Companies, was sent out on a prolonged "search and destroy" mission, Operation Abilene. It was a bad time for Charlie Company to engage with the Viet Cong. The company was down to 134 men, due to soldiers who'd recently been killed or wounded, or were on leave.

De la O, with the radio on his back, stuck close to his commander. It was a nerve-racking job: the VC always tried to kill the radio operator to break off communications.

On the morning of April 11, 1966, Charlie Company was separated from Alpha and Bravo. Charlie Company was spread out in a long line in the dense jungle vegetation. At noon, de la O took a call from the far end of Charlie Company reporting suspicious movement nearby. De la O relayed back the commander's order to patrol and see what they could find. Long minutes passed, then de la O's radio crackled with static: it was the radio operator reporting back, hysterical. De la O could hear men yelling, machine-gun fire, and loud explosions. Suddenly the radio operator screamed, and the line went dead.

Charlie Company scrambled to set up a perimeter to defend themselves. Sniper fire turned to machine-gun and mortar fire. By 2:00 p.m., they were surrounded, totally cut off from Alpha and Bravo.

They were outnumbered by a crack Viet Cong battalion, and dead and wounded Americans were soon scattered throughout the jungle undergrowth. "It was horrible," said one soldier. "I've never heard such screaming in my life. Many of the wounded were yelling for their mothers. Some . . . were calling for God."

De la O stuck close to the commander, who fired off messages for de la O to relay on the radio. Small artillery fire whined around them, and grenades exploded, throwing plants and dirt into the air. The commander suddenly went down, hit by a bullet. De la O dropped his radio and pulled off his first aid pack. He fumbled for a bandage to staunch the commander's bleeding. "You better save that for yourself," the commander said. *Oh my God*, thought de la O, *what is he telling me?*

US helicopters hover over American soldiers, 1965. The Vietnam War was often referred to as the "helicopter war," as the US relied heavily on them to attack, resupply, reinforce troops, and evacuate wounded.

Medic Andrew J. Brown, pistol drawn for protection, crawls through the jungle to treat an injured paratrooper despite sniper fire and a live grenade lying nearby, 1965.

The Viet Cong moved in tighter, forcing Charlie Company into small groups, cutting them off from one another. Word passed through the company to get ready: the Viet Cong were coming in for an all-out assault. De la O and another infantry-man ended up next to each other. They piled extra ammunition and a sack of grenades nearby, and made sure their machetes were within easy reach. "We figured this was it," said de la O.

With death so close, something happened to de la O while he waited. "They say your life goes before you," de la O said. "I finally experienced it. I saw some of the people that I had wronged when I was growing up, and disrespected. And all their faces came in front of me." There was no time now for remorse. All he could do was try to stay alive.

Soon it was pitch-black. De la O literally couldn't see his hand in front of his face. Fortunately, the Americans had plenty of artillery support. "When it started getting dark, they started shooting these illumination rounds," de la O said. "It would explode up in the air and then it had, like, a little parachute on it, so as it was coming down, it would light up the area. So we had some light. But then as soon as it died out—boom, Chuckie would start firing again."

In the early morning, Bravo Company was finally able to come to their aid. With the arrival of fresh forces, the VC disappeared into the jungle. Bravo soldiers took over. They blew a large clearing in the jungle using C-4 explosive. Choppers arrived and took out the wounded, the dead, and the survivors.

The operation decimated Charlie Company. Seventy-one men were wounded, and thirty-six killed.

New recruits, fresh from the United States, were rushed to the company. For a few weeks, everyone was busy teaching newcomers the ropes. They were green and scared, and had no idea how to protect themselves or work as part of a unit. If they weren't trained correctly, they could get killed right away, and put other men at risk.

De la O hit it off with one of the new medics, Jimmy Stamey. He was outgoing, fun-loving, with a huge smile and sense of humor. But on patrol or during an operation, he was serious, and absolutely fearless. "When someone yelled 'medic,'" said de la O, "we knew Jimmy would come a-running." De la O was acutely aware how critical a competent, brave medic was out in the field. On patrol with Stamey, he knew everyone would get the best care possible, and fast. Out in the field, they weren't fighting to protect democracy, or the United States, or any ideal. They were fighting for their lives, and their buddies' lives.

During downtime, Stamey and de la O talked about their homes and families, girls and sports. They shared private thoughts about what they wanted to do when they got back to "the world." Their biggest bond was rock and roll. No matter what Stamey was doing—standing in chow lines, cleaning his equipment, writing letters home—he was always singing. He had a rich voice, and being from Alabama, he had a soft way of drawing out his vowels when he sang. De la O loved to hear him sing the Beatles' "Anna (Go to Him)" and "Up on the Roof" by the Drifters. Sometimes de la O would join in, even though Stamey would rib him about how off-key he was.

Toward the end of his year in Vietnam, de la O was no longer put on long operations. He was brought back to the rear area to acclimatize and get cleaned up. The last weekend in September, he was told the time had come: he would be leaving Vietnam the next day.

That night, Stamey gave de la O two photographs of himself in his high-school football uniform. On one, he carefully wrote out his address, and they promised to stay in touch.

Marine Claiborne L. Shaw takes a break next to a sign showing the distance to Oakland, California, 1966. Shortly after this photo was taken Shaw was killed. He is honored on the Wall, Panel 10E, Row 11.

Flag-draped coffins of American servicemen are placed in a plane for the trip back to the United States, 1965. Funeral services were held at the Saigon Airport and each casket was pinned with Vietnamese and American medals.

It was the early hours of the morning when de la O finally made it all the way back to his parents' house in Minnesota. He fell into an exhausted sleep, and woke up to a house that was full of aunts and uncles, cousins and old friends, all eager to hear about his year. What was it like in Vietnam? Where had he been wounded? Could they see his Purple Heart? How many enemies had he killed?

There was no way de la O could talk about his time in Vietnam. "It just didn't feel right, being home," he said. Everything should have been okay, but it wasn't. He called an uncle in Chicago who'd been in combat in World War II and asked if he could come for a visit. He spent weeks in his uncle's quiet apartment before he was ready to go back home.

President Johnson and Martin Luther King Jr. in a meeting at the White House, 1966.

AMERICA: PROTESTOR

MARTIN LUTHER KING JR.
JANUARY 1967—OCTOBER 1967

"Never again will I be silent on an issue that is destroying the soul of our nation and destroying thousands and thousands of little children in Vietnam."

IN JANUARY 1967, Martin Luther King Jr. flew to Jamaica for a quiet, month-long visit. He'd promised to finish a book he was writing and needed to get away from the daily, ongoing demands of leadership in the civil rights movement. Late one night, after a long day of writing, he pulled a copy of *Ramparts* magazine from a box of books he'd brought with him. A twenty-four-page photo essay, "The Children of Vietnam," caught his attention: page after page of Vietnamese children, their small bodies riddled with shrapnel, limbs maimed by bombs, skin and flesh deeply burned by American chemical weapons, napalm and phosphorous.

The vulnerable, grievously wounded children were haunting. How could he be so passionately against violence at home, and yet say so little about Vietnam? How many more innocent children like these were going to be hurt and killed? Many leaders in the civil rights struggle were afraid to speak out against the war, fearing they would be branded as unpatriotic, and the civil rights movement would be damaged. King wrestled with his conscience: were these legitimate reasons to remain silent?

Then there was President Johnson, who'd worked so steadily with King on civil rights. It was no secret Johnson expected utter loyalty to all his policies in return.

King was painfully aware he could—*would*—irrevocably destroy his partnership with the president by unequivocally speaking out against the war. Would an all-out rupture between the two of them cause the whole civil rights movement to lose ground?

King already had a meeting scheduled with Johnson when he returned. He canceled it, and then called off another. It was unprecedented on his part—he had always been eager to have the president's ear. But King needed time to reflect and strategize without Johnson's notorious arm-twisting.

Johnson had an unerring instinct for political betrayal and knew something was going on. It made him deeply uneasy. "He's canceled two meetings with me," Johnson said querulously to an aide. "I don't understand it." As much as King needed the president, the reverse was also true. Frustration and anger were boiling over in the largely African American inner cities, leading to riots and brutal confrontations between the protestors and police. In some cities, the National Guard was being mobilized in an attempt to bring order to the rioting. Young militant leaders were emerging in the civil rights struggle, making Johnson nervous. He depended on King's nonviolent agenda to be a voice of moderation and restraint.

Free of any pressure from the White House, King gathered his thoughts and prayed for guidance. He acknowledged to himself that for too long, he'd ignored his conscience. He often preached that looking away from evil and remaining silent was, in effect, supporting the evil. No matter what the cost, he decided he had to step forward, "if I was to erase my name from the bombs which fall over North or South Vietnam, from the canisters of napalm." Antiwar protests had been steadily getting larger as Johnson expanded the war effort, and King told his advisors he planned to speak at an upcoming New York City demonstration.

His advisors were vehemently opposed. They didn't trust the white radicals who dominated the peace movement, and they didn't want civil rights linked with hippie protestors. King's advisors argued and pleaded with him, but he was done soul-searching. It was time for him to publicly, firmly, come out against the war. His advisors begged him to at least speak somewhere he could have the podium to himself to carefully lay out his thoughts and feelings. King agreed.

On April 4, the pews in the Riverside Church in New York City were filled to

overflowing. More people spilled out the doorway and onto the sidewalk to listen on loudspeakers set up outside. King began his speech, "Beyond Vietnam," by acknowledging he was moved to "break the betrayal of my own silences and to speak from the burnings of my own heart." He laid out the terrible injustice of black and white men fighting "in brutal solidarity," only to come home to a country where they could rarely live on the same block. As middle- and upper-class young men were much more likely to get a deferment from the draft, King noted how the draft ended up unfairly targeting the poor—white and black alike. He didn't stop with just the effect on Americans. The children of Vietnam, who'd forced him to grapple with his conscience, needed and deserved to be free from falling bombs and searing napalm.

Nor was King content to just enumerate the tragedies for Vietnamese civilians and American servicemen. He had five specific, concrete actions he believed America needed to pursue immediately: stop bombing, declare a cease-fire, curtail our military buildup in nearby countries, accept that we needed to negotiate with the North

Vietnamese, and set a date to remove our troops. It was a shocking, groundbreaking speech, especially from a civil rights leader.

King expected a backlash, but he wasn't prepared for the storm of criticism that came at him from all directions. Moderate black leaders quickly distanced themselves from him, saying it was crucial the focus remain solely on civil rights. *The New York Times* and *The Washington Post*, two of the most widely read newspapers in the country, were scathing. "Dr. King's Error" headlined *The New York Times* on April 7. The article claimed King's decision "to divert the energies of the civil rights movement to the Vietnam issue is both wasteful and self-defeating." *The Washington Post*'s editorial, "A Tragedy," insisted King had betrayed his cause. Critics said he had no right to speak on foreign affairs. He should "stay in his place," a derisive way of putting down both his race and his domestic civil rights work.

King kept speaking out. The American war effort had made Johnson's Great Society a myth, King said, and had created a "troubled and confused society."

As King anticipated, Johnson was furious. After all he had done for King and his movement, he felt deeply wounded by King's betrayal. It meant the end of any phone calls or White House visits with the president. But unbeknownst to King, Johnson went significantly further than cutting off contact. For several years, the head of the Federal Bureau of Investigation (FBI), J. Edgar Hoover, had been eager to prove to the president that King was a dangerous man with Communist affiliations. Johnson had rebuffed Hoover in the past, but now the president was willing to listen to his reports that King was controlled by powerful Communists. Hoover incorrectly believed both the peace movement and the civil rights movement were Communist attempts to take over the entire United States.

Violence kept escalating in American inner cities, and tensions reached a boiling point in the middle of the hot, restless summer of 1967. On July 22, a group of friends gathered in Detroit at a "blind pig," an unlicensed bar, to drink and welcome two black servicemen back from Vietnam. The men had served their country and were home safe. In the early hours of the morning, the vice squad moved in on the illegal bar and arrested everyone, setting off days of rioting and looting. The National Guard was unable to restore calm, and the president ordered nearly 5,000 army troops onto

The National Guard patrols a Detroit street after police raided a blind pig, setting off riots, 1967. Numerous fires started by firebombs created a smoky haze.

the streets of Detroit. Many of them had recently returned from Vietnam. Now they were being commanded to turn their guns on their fellow citizens.

For five days and nights, news coverage of burning buildings, tanks, and armed troops focused on American streets, not Vietnamese villages and jungles. By the time the riot was over, forty-three people were dead, and more than a thousand were injured.

The rioting devastated King. In August he appeared on national television to explain his position. "The tragedy is that we are today engaged in two wars and we are losing both," he said. "We are losing the war against poverty here at home; we are losing the war in Vietnam morally and politically. I think we are losing this war at home precisely because of the energies, the resources, the money, and all of the other things that we are putting in that tragic, unjust, evil, brutal, senseless war in Vietnam."

The unending fight for justice both in black communities and in Vietnam exhausted King. He fell into a deeply reflective, melancholy mood. But he refused to back down from his beliefs, saying, "If I am the last, lone voice speaking for nonviolence, that I will do."

VIETNAM:
MACHINE GUNNER

HENRY ALLEN
IN COUNTRY APRIL 1967—MAY 1968

"When I saw my comrades dying, then I took on a real mean spirit, a fighting spirit. I was seeking revenge. All I wanted to do was look for the enemy and find him and destroy him. Not capture him, but destroy him."

WHEN HENRY ALLEN joined the military, it never occurred to him that he would end up serving as a machine gunner in Vietnam. Allen was deeply committed to civil rights and had been trained in nonviolence by some of the movement's greatest leaders, including Martin Luther King Jr. The M60 machine gun assignment posed a terrible problem for him. So Allen came up with a secret, highly improbable strategy for getting through Vietnam. "I was going to tote this machine gun for a year and I would never have to shoot it," he said. "That's what my heart was on. It never worked out that way."

Allen had grown up dirt-poor, in a three-room house with no running water. Some days there was no food to eat, and Allen and his best friend, Louis Taylor, would roam the streets looking for old cans and bottles to turn in for a few cents. But no matter how hungry Allen was, he loved learning and school, and playing on the East Selma baseball team with Taylor.

Unlike many towns in the South, Allen's neighborhood in Selma, Alabama, was racially mixed. His white next-door neighbors, the Peppers, thought he was smart and capable. When Allen needed glasses, Mr. Pepper bought them for him. In tenth grade, Allen was hired by Mr. Pepper to help in his electronic-repair business, fixing radios and TVs. But there were plenty of things Allen couldn't do with the Peppers. Segregation laws and customs in the South between the two races were strictly enforced. "We could work together," said Allen, "but we could not go to school together, or go to the movies together. We couldn't do anything in public together."

Allen was a junior when civil rights leaders from the Student Nonviolent Coordinating Committee (SNCC) moved to town to register African Americans to vote. The SNCC activists reached out to teenagers, saying they could nonviolently fight for the change their parents deserved, for the world they wanted to have as adults. The activists asked thought-provoking questions: Why do you go to a separate school from whites? Why aren't you allowed to sit at the lunch counters? Allen quickly became committed to SNCC's nonviolent ideals: always meet hatred with love, and strive to eliminate evil, not destroy the evildoer.

In twelfth grade, Allen and Taylor had to figure out what to do after high school. They had seen what happened to seniors at their all-black school. As soon as they dropped out or graduated, they got a notice to report to the draft board. They were sent off to boot camp, where they didn't know another soul. Next stop: Vietnam.

Neither Allen nor Taylor wanted to get drafted. Would it be better if they enlisted in the military on the "buddy program" that allowed friends to go through boot camp together? At least they'd be with each other, instead of being away from everyone they knew.

But after listening to the SNCC leaders, Allen didn't want to fight to liberate the Vietnamese from Communism, with all the work there was to do at home for civil rights. "I had deep feelings because of the fact that I wasn't even free," Allen said. "My community wasn't free. And I was going to go ten thousand miles to fight for someone else's freedom?" It wasn't right.

He decided he'd go to the nearby two-year college in Birmingham, Alabama. As long as he was in school, he'd have a student deferment from the draft. Taylor signed up for the Marines.

During Allen's first year in Birmingham, Martin Luther King Jr. came to Selma, bringing national attention to the voting-rights campaign. Allen took the bus back and forth, eager to listen to King and to keep marching as a foot soldier in the struggle for racial equality.

After Allen finished his two years of college, the army quickly reclassified him 1-A, available for military service. Allen decided not to fight it. He would just get his service done and then he could move on with his life. In November 1966, he was inducted into the army and the following April was sent to Vietnam. Like all new arrivals at a get-to-know-you reception in Vietnam, Allen was asked where he was from. "It was no secret about Selma," he said. "Everybody knew about Selma. They said, 'What are you doing over here? You got a war going on back in your hometown.'" It quickly turned to ribbing. "'Matter of fact,' they said, 'you should already be a good soldier. You're already prepared for war.'"

Officers asked for volunteers to drive trucks around the base. Allen raised his hand. He was given a wheelbarrow and told to collect human waste from the privies. White volunteers were assigned to the trucks.

Allen was sent to Charlie Company, 1st Battalion, 2nd Infantry Regiment, headquartered north of Saigon. Known as the Black Scarf Battalion, the members proudly wore black scarves on their necks. Allen was put in the weapons platoon as an ammo bearer for the M60 machine gun. The job was often given to the new guy in the unit. It was brutally hard work walking through the jungle loaded down with bandoliers of heavy ammunition.

Every morning, Allen made sure the small Bible he'd been given in basic training was in his left-hand pocket, carefully wrapped in plastic to stay dry. "I kept my military Bible with me every day. My favorite was the twenty-seventh psalm. 'The Lord is my light and my salvation. Whom shall I fear? The Lord is the stronghold of my life. Of whom shall I be afraid?'"

On his first assignment, Allen was sent out for a night patrol with his unit. They were flown deep into the jungle and set down in an area known to be crawling with VC. The Americans set up camp, putting out one-sided explosive claymore mines along the perimeter for protection. If the enemy came close, they would set off the mines.

Under the cover of darkness, the VC crept in silently and turned the mines around. When the Americans finally heard the VC and detonated the mines, hundreds of small steel balls exploded back at them, tearing into their flesh. The assistant gunner was badly injured, and Allen was promoted to his position. It wasn't long until the machine gunner was killed on another night mission. Allen was promoted again, and assigned to a new crew. Now he was the one in charge of releasing the machine gun's deadly power of 550 rounds per minute.

"I got on the deep side," he said, "real deep. I didn't want to shoot that machine gun. That's the deep side." It went against everything he'd been trained in by SNCC and King. He was thrown into more turmoil when he heard that back in the United States, King had publicly come out against the war. What was he doing here fighting the North Vietnamese?

But Allen wasn't a foot soldier in the civil rights struggle anymore. He was in the US Army now, bound by the rules of the military. He had been ordered out many times on "search and destroy" missions after planes had sprayed the herbicide Agent Orange to kill any vegetation in their path. "They also used napalm before we went in an area," Allen said. "We'd walk through and there would still be gel on the ground." He'd been in firefights, seen the men he was with injured and killed. Not only would he be risking his life in a fight by not using his machine gun, but also he'd jeopardize the lives of the men he served with.

While he struggled within himself, Allen and nine others were ordered to go out in the jungle to spend the night. There were rumors that an NVA battalion was gathering. Allen thought the order was insane. They were being sent out as bait for the enemy to lure them into an attack, to flush them out of hiding. As far as Allen could tell, it was a complete suicide mission, the ten of them being dropped into the jungle next to a battalion of hundreds of enemy soldiers.

Should he refuse to follow orders? He knew exactly what would happen if he did.

American planes spray fields with Agent Orange, 1969. Both jungles and rice fields suspected of being used by the Viet Cong were targeted. Agent Orange was later linked to cancer and birth defects in Vietnamese and Americans who were heavily exposed to it.

He'd be sent to Long Binh Jail, the American stockade on Long Binh Post, twelve miles northeast of Saigon. Notorious for overcrowding and violence, the prison was known by its initials, LBJ, in a sarcastic tip of the hat to the president. "I felt like going to prison would be of more value to my life than going out there and getting killed," he said. He prayed hard for guidance.

"At the last minute, the spirit told me to go," he said. "My mind changed." *Don't disobey orders*, he thought. *Everything is going to be all right.* Allen put his trust in God, and got ready. He and the other men—six white and three black—loaded up with weapons. Allen made sure he had his Bible, as always, in his pocket.

Through the long, still night, they took turns on watch, ears straining to hear the slightest sounds of movement: a twig snapping, a branch swishing against clothing, the unmistakable sound of a metallic click, a human whisper. Allen was also listening for the reassuring noises of animals: the whine of mosquitoes, the whir of crickets, the scurry of rats in the underbrush. If all noises abruptly stopped, it meant the animals—all of them—were suddenly on alert. There were probably VC moving toward them in the darkness. They'd have seconds, maybe a minute, before all hell broke loose.

During his watch, Allen thought about his old gun crew, the injuries and deaths he'd seen. The buddy he'd trained with back in the United States who'd stepped on a mine and blown off his foot. The day he was dropped into a hot LZ—a landing zone under fire—by helicopter, and the men on either side of him were shot, one in the upper shoulder, one three times in the chest. There was no time to mourn, no compassion for the wounded. "When we went out on operations, you knew not everybody was coming back," he said. "It affected you. I would try not to get on a personal basis with people." The more distance he had, the easier it was.

Allen stayed awake all night, talking to the Lord and listening for the enemy. As dawn slowly turned the dense jungle from pitch-black to gray, birds began their melodic calls. They had made it through the long night.

Days later, Bravo Company walked right into a horseshoe ambush set up by a battalion of four or five hundred NVA. Charlie Company was mobilized and sent to back them up.

Allen carried his heavy machine gun and as much ammunition as he could handle. He told his assistant and ammo bearer to each bring a spare machine gun for him, and as much ammo as they could possibly carry. The compassion and nonviolence Allen had been taught was totally gone now. "Being a combat soldier makes you real mean.

I was extremely mean," he said. The North Vietnamese were killing his comrades. He would destroy as many as he could. The army wanted a body count of enemy dead—he'd provide it.

Allen set up his machine gun and started firing. Behind him, his buddies were busy keeping their heads down and loading the other two guns as fast as they could. As soon as Allen ran out of ammo, he would toss his red-hot empty gun back, and a new one would be thrust into his hands. "They kept loading, and I kept firing," he said. All around Allen was utter chaos as the Americans were picked off by the seasoned NVA troops. A soldier next to Allen went down, and when the medic belly-crawled over to him, he was killed. Allen just kept firing. Finally, under the cover of darkness, the enemy suddenly disappeared, like ghosts.

Over the next months, Allen's squad was repeatedly sent into the bush for three or four weeks at a stretch. "We didn't change clothes," he said. "We wore the same clothes. Leeches all over your body. It was a tough life." After a day of search and de-stroy, he was dead tired at night. It didn't matter to him that they slept on the ground. "I could sleep in a pen with a hog and have a good night's sleep," Allen said. "It didn't matter how I slept."

Sometimes the biggest enemy was sheer, unremitting thirst. On one long operation, Allen was burning up with thirst, his mouth parched dry, his tongue swollen. His squad came to a muddy stream draining a rice paddy. Allen could see the water was contaminated. "There were dead bodies in the water," he said. "There was everything in the water you could dream of." He'd watched friends weakened and exhausted by unrelenting diarrhea out in the field. He'd seen others get hepatitis from bad water. "I had three iodine tablets. I took my canteen cup and I looked into heaven at our Father in heaven. 'I'm thirsty,' I said. 'I'm gonna drink this water today believing that you are going to purify this water.'" He drank until his thirst was slaked, protected by iodine and a prayer.

Overleaf: US soldiers are soaked by a downpour as they carefully fill their canteens with fresh rainwater, 1968.

Back at the base, Allen kept his personal pledge not to get close to any of the other men. He would eat hot meals, stand for long minutes in a shower, read his Bible, and wait for mail call. "The first package I got was from the Peppers," he said. "Then the second was from them." Far away from home, his heart hardened and ruthless, he knew they were thinking of him. "Those packages let me know exactly how much they cared." His Bible and the packages were the only time he had any feelings other than meanness and a desire for revenge.

Allen made it out of battle after battle. "When they say a cat has nine lives, I thought that God gave me ten," he said. But after months of fighting, an American bomb dropped near him, and threw a chunk of metal into his pants, hitting him right in the backside. His whole body instantly felt numb. "Diaz, look behind me," he yelled to his assistant gunner. "I think my whole back end is blown off. I'm afraid to look." Allen was beside himself with fear. "I don't wanna look, I don't wanna look," he said over and over again. Diaz hurried over. "He busts out laughing," said Allen. "'Your ass is still there,' Diaz said."

While Allen was recovering in the field hospital, his platoon leader came in to award him a Purple Heart. Allen told the officer he wouldn't take it. His platoon leader was shocked. No one ever refused a Purple Heart. He told Allen he couldn't turn it down. Allen stubbornly repeated himself. "I'm not going to accept it," he said.

Too many times, Allen had seen up close how racism worked in the army. Not on the front lines—the men worked closely together to make sure everyone survived. But a few months earlier, Allen had been in a desperate firefight along with two white guys from his platoon. One had been awarded the Distinguished Service Cross, and one the Silver Star, both high honors. There was zero recognition for Allen. "It was all determined by your platoon leader, who 99 percent of the time was white," said Allen. He knew the two soldiers had been good friends with the platoon leader. "Those guys were all buddy-buddy, and he was writing reports up that made sure they got their awards," said Allen. He had taken the same risks and shown the same bravery as the other two men. It was humiliating to be offered a Purple Heart now, and he wasn't going to let his platoon leader insult him like that.

Soldiers at a memorial service for Martin Luther King Jr. in Da Nang, 1968. The chaplain eulogized King's commitment to nonviolence.

Despite his pledge not to get close to anyone, a tragic loss hit Allen on March 6, 1968. His childhood friend from Selma, Louis Taylor, was just days away from finishing his tour when his plane was shot down and everyone aboard died.

More bad news followed a month later. Allen was standing with his regiment at the base of the Black Virgin Mountain. Everyone was nervous. "We were going to do something very dangerous," said Allen. "We were going to assault a mountain with the enemy at the top." As they waited to be sent out, word came over the radio that King had just been killed. A shock wave ran through the troops. "When he got shot," said one infantryman, "people were walking around going, 'What are we doing here when they're killing one of the greatest men the world has ever known back there? Why are we fighting here?'"

Officers recognized the troops were angry and unruly. They were in no mood to mount the assault. The operation was canceled, and Allen's company was sent back to

The oldest and most respected man in his village with his great-grandchildren, 1970. American soldiers rarely found able-bodied men in the villages, as they would flee or hide to avoid the possibility they would be interrogated. Because the Americans couldn't tell who was fighting for the Viet Cong, they were suspicious of all but the oldest men.

base camp. King's death hit Allen hard. It was a bitter reminder that everything King had taught him had been wiped out by his time in the military.

They were soon in combat again, and after a prolonged, bloody battle, Allen was ordered to guard a pile of several hundred dead NVA soldiers. Americans went through the pockets of the dead Vietnamese, searching for papers, photographs, maps: anything that might provide information to military intelligence.

"I spent days guarding those bodies," he said. "I saw pictures of their families. And then I began to realize they had wives, they had children." Allen thought about the dead men, their loved ones, their commitment to their country and government. For so long the NVA had been just "the enemy." *They are fighting for a cause, I am fighting for a cause,* he realized. *They're human. In the eyes of God, we are all brothers.*

Something profound shifted in Allen. "That brought my humanity back," he said. "It was gone. I had lost it."

Still, it wasn't quite that simple. Now that he recognized in his heart how he had changed, he had to shift his mind-set, his angry, mean-spirited ways. He finished out his year in Vietnam in turmoil, relying on his Bible and his faith in God, just hoping to survive. On May 5, 1968, he boarded a plane, took a window seat, and stared out at the lush green country he was about to leave.

As the plane taxied down the runway, the enemy suddenly let off a burst of rocket fire. Peering out the window, Allen could see rockets speeding toward them. *God, let this plane taxi the runway!* he prayed. The plane lifted off, rose hard and fast, and cleared the rockets.

When he arrived in Oakland, California, Allen walked off the plane and dropped to his knees. "I kissed the ground and I promised God I would serve him for the rest of my life. He did a lot for me."

Allen couldn't wait to shed his uniform and get into regular clothes. It would take him several days to get back to Selma on the train and the bus, and he wanted to relax. A white officer stopped him and recommended he stay in uniform. As he traveled through the South, belligerent whites might give him trouble. Hopefully they'd respect the uniform.

The advice was well-meaning, but infuriating. He'd just spent a whole year of his life fighting for his country. He'd been in mortal danger repeatedly, been injured, watched buddies die. Allen stayed in uniform, jumpy and on edge, until he made it back home.

AMERICA:
PRESIDENT AND COMMANDER IN CHIEF

LYNDON B. JOHNSON
OCTOBER 1967—FEBRUARY 1968

"Every night when I fell asleep I would see myself tied to the ground in the middle of a long, open space. In the distance I could hear the voices of thousands of people. They were all shouting at me and running toward me: 'Coward! Traitor! Weakling!'"

PRESIDENT JOHNSON AGONIZED every time he had to send more men to fight in Vietnam, but ground combat was a critical part of his "search and destroy" strategy of using troops to kill off the enemy one by one. While escalating the bombing, he continually increased troop levels. A secret attempt at peace negotiations with the North Vietnamese was going nowhere.

To make sure he didn't miss a single piece of news coming out of Vietnam and reaching the American public, Johnson had installed three televisions in the Oval Office, side by side. With a remote control in his hand, he watched all three concurrent news programs every night, raising the volume on any war coverage.

The strategy in Vietnam wasn't going well. Territory was lost, then hard-won, then lost again. Squalid refugee camps were crowded with displaced villagers. It was impossible to determine if farmers were Viet Cong or not, and an insistence on a high body count number

Vietnam War protestors at the March on the Pentagon, 1967.

President Johnson watches all three nightly news broadcasts at the same time in the Oval Office, 1967.
He had a special console built to hold the televisions.

contributed to innocent civilian deaths. Despite the constant search and destroy, there was always a steady flow of fresh troops from North Vietnam.

At home, public support for the war was slowly eroding, and Johnson's fear that American troop morale would slip as the war dragged on was proving painfully correct.

Johnson felt beleaguered on all sides. "This is not Johnson's war," he yelled at a journalist who'd come to interview him in the White House. "This is America's war. If I drop dead tomorrow, this war will still be with you."

Protestors didn't buy it. They blamed the president, flooding onto city streets and campuses. Antiwar activists organized their biggest protest yet in October 1967. Fifty thousand people made their way to Washington, DC. They gathered at the Lincoln Memorial to listen to speeches, then many of them marched on the Pentagon, headquarters of the United States Department of Defense. The protestors were against the war, against the draft, and against Johnson. "Hey, hey, LBJ," chanted the marchers, "how many kids did you kill today?"

The president decided to mount a "Success Offensive." He had General Westmoreland fly back from Vietnam in November to convince Americans the war was going well. "I am absolutely certain that, whereas in 1965 the enemy was winning, today he is certainly losing," Westmoreland said. "The enemy's hopes are bankrupt." He projected an air of confidence, telling an interviewer, "I hope they try something, because we are looking for a fight."

By the end of 1967, Johnson had nearly half a million troops in Vietnam.

Privately, Westmoreland confided to Johnson that the North Vietnamese were definitely up to something. He wasn't sure just what it was, but it looked like they meant to mount a huge attack on Khe Sanh, the American base next to the Laotian border.

Westmoreland's military intelligence was tragically incomplete. In the early-morning hours of January 31, 1968, more than 80,000 NVA troops and VC launched the Tet Offensive, an all-out invasion of South Vietnam. They simultaneously attacked nearly every major city and many of the military bases. For weeks they had been silently infiltrating South Vietnam, and they struck with a coordinated fury that shocked everyone.

President Johnson tried to downplay the massive attack at a news conference on February 2, saying "a few bandits can do that in any city." But it quickly became clear that the Communist forces were disciplined and committed as they wreaked carnage on both military and civilian groups.

As American casualties shot up, debilitating insomnia kept Johnson awake at night, prowling the White House halls in his bathrobe and slippers. He made frequent trips down to the Situation Room in the White House basement to hear the latest news.

On February 18, weekly US casualty figures hit their highest number ever in the war—a staggering 543 Americans were killed and 2,547 wounded in just seven days of fighting. General Westmoreland requested an additional 206,000 American troops. He wanted the president to expand ground operations into nearby Laos and Cambodia, and massively increase bombing of North Vietnam.

The request unleashed bitter disagreements within the administration. Some advisors wanted more bombing, other suggested calling up the Army Reserves to fight. Within the privacy of the White House, there were even discussions if it would become necessary to use nuclear weapons.

Johnson didn't want nuclear weapons on the table, or calling up the Army Reserves. He was afraid of escalating tensions with the Soviet and Chinese Communists by increased bombing. At home, he knew the American public would be vehemently against putting even more American lives at risk by sending in several hundred thousand more American troops. Again and again, he went down to the Situation Room to stay abreast of the latest fighting. Appalled by the carnage, distressed by conflicting advice, he was sure of only one thing: he couldn't let a democracy fall into Communist hands. He was not going to be the president who lost the war and let that happen.

Across the United States, millions of Americans were glued to their televisions for the evening news reports, and stunned at the savage fighting they saw on their screens. It was shocking to see the enemy they'd been assured was nearly defeated strike with such ferocity.

In bloody street-to-street fighting, the North Vietnamese Army and VC forces were pushed back by the Americans and South Vietnamese. Militarily, the Tet Offensive was a win for South Vietnam and the United States. But for President Johnson, it was a profound personal and political failure.

Walter Cronkite, the popular anchorman for the *CBS Evening News*, had long been a solid supporter of Johnson's. But the Tet Offensive shook his confidence in the administration. How could this have happened? What was going on in Vietnam? Cronkite decided to go see for himself. He took only a cameraman and a soundman so he could move quickly from place to place. In Vietnam, he interviewed all kinds of people: soldiers, rice farmers, orphans, generals, and even the South Vietnamese president, Nguyen Van Thieu. Cronkite spoke extensively with journalists and reporters who'd been in Vietnam for months or years, and asked for their honest opinions.

Anchorman Walter Cronkite conducts an interview in Hue, Vietnam, for his CBS News Special Report on the war, 1968.

Back in the United States, Cronkite put together *Report from Vietnam: Who, What, When, Where, Why?* and rushed it onto the air on February 27, 1968. It was not part of the evening news, but was highlighted as a prime-time CBS News Special Report. "To say that we are mired in stalemate seems the only realistic, yet unsatisfactory, conclusion," reported Cronkite. It was time, he said, for the United States to negotiate with the North Vietnamese, "not as victors, but as an honorable people who lived up to their pledge to defend democracy and did the best they could."

Johnson was traveling on the official presidential plane, Air Force One, when he was told about the Special Report. "If I've lost Cronkite," he blurted out, "I've lost the country."

He was right. It was a terrible time to lose the confidence of the American public. Johnson was in the last year of his four-year term and would soon need to seek reelection.

Marines pull a wounded soldier to safety during the Tet Offensive, 1968.

VIETNAM: MEDIC

TOM KELLEY
IN COUNTRY DECEMBER 1967—DECEMBER 1968

"I saved hundreds of lives, I know I did. But that is very cold comfort. It is the ones I lost that I remember. In my nightmares I see the faces of people who died."

ON CHRISTMAS DAY 1967, Tom Kelley's plane touched down in Vietnam, and he stepped into a wave of heat, chaos, and noise. Orders were barked at the new arrivals as they tried to figure out where they were supposed to be, and what they were supposed to be doing. Soldiers who'd served their year were waiting for flights out with an exhausted, used-up look in their eyes.

After boot camp, Kelley had been trained as an infantry medic. It hadn't surprised him that army testing had shown he would make a good medic. When he was growing up, his mother loved animals, and they always had cats and at least one dog. His mother had a hot temper, and boyfriends and husbands came and went as they moved from one small California town to another. The steadiest thing in Kelley's life was their pets, and he decided early on he wanted to be a veterinarian. As soon as he enrolled in college, Kelley had started pre-veterinarian courses. But by the spring of his second year, he had to drop out to earn money to continue. The Selective Service caught up with him, and he was drafted.

Tom Kelley (left) and a friend in medical training at Fort Sam Houston in San Antonio, Texas, 1967.

After a few weeks in Vietnam, Kelley was assigned to the 440th Medical Detachment at the 91st Evacuation Hospital at Tuy Hoa. He was also assigned his buddy—a man named Bruce Pawlak. "He was threatening," said Kelley. "Muscular. Tattooed. A hunky guy." Pawlak was also brilliant. To relax, he read science fiction and studied Einstein's theory of relativity.

Kelley quickly learned to hear the far-off *whap-whap-whap* of the rotors as the medical Dust Off helicopter approached. He and Pawlak would hurry out to the cement landing pad by the hospital to pull loaded stretchers off the choppers and rush the injured into the ER. The two instantly formed a tight bond: both were willing to work hard and make tough decisions to save wounded infantrymen.

Combat medicine was torn flesh, gaping belly wounds, splintered bones, burns, blood, and agony. It was way more than Kelley could handle stone-cold sober. By the end of his first few weeks at the hospital, he was smoking marijuana and hanging out with the dope-smokers.

Kelley had been in country for just over a month when the Tet Offensive began. From the very first day, casualties poured into the 91st Evacuation Hospital, overwhelming the medical personnel. "The helicopters are landing," said Kelley. "We're off-loading the wounded into the ER. We're going back and a new helicopter is landing, and we're taking them to the ER."

All sixteen available medics were ordered to keep working. Stretchers—also called litters—were brought in at a run from ambulances and truck beds. There was no time to sleep, no time to even rest. Every ten or twelve hours, Kelley and the other medics would be handed a Dexedrine pill, an amphetamine used by the military to ward off exhaustion. It wasn't a case of being offered Dexedrine. It was a direct order: Take it. Men are dying. You've got work to do.

Helicopters off-loaded the wounded so fast, there was no room left inside the ER. Kelley and Pawlak started parking the injured men in the covered walk space alongside the building. Soon there were fifty or sixty stretchers jammed together outside the ER.

The dead were taken straight to Graves Registration. There was no time to process them, note where the casualties were from, or even what unit they belonged to. The medics had to just stack the bodies and get back to work. "The Graves Registration was so full," Kelley said, "you couldn't even get in the door."

As soon as Kelley had an injured man off the helicopter, he grabbed the "casualty tag" pinned on the guy's shirt and read it. Out in the field, medics had scrawled a rough assessment on the tag, and jotted down the time of the helicopter pickup. Stuck in the patient's lapel were empty syrettes—syringes prefilled with morphine—to let the hospital crew know how much morphine he'd already been given.

Kelley hated to see tags with a black cross mark written on them. It meant the medic thought the patient wouldn't survive his injuries. Possibly he could be saved with surgery—if the doctors had time—but at least he could be kept comfortable until he died.

Kelley had been up for more than thirty hours when a new first lieutenant arrived in the chaotic ER. He ordered everyone to "lock heels"—stand at attention and listen, eyes straight ahead. Kelley could feel blood squelching around in his boots, and his uniform was crusted with fresh and dried blood, sweat, dirt, and vomit. Even wired on amphetamines, he was in a haze of exhaustion.

The medics, jammed between litters of critically injured men, stood at attention in front of the lieutenant. Kelley could hear a helicopter landing outside. "All right," barked the lieutenant. "You two here will be litter team A." He gestured to two of the medics. "You will be litter team B." Kelley couldn't believe what the lieutenant was saying. It was straight out of some military medical training course. *Who is this officious little chrome-dome?* he thought. Before Pawlak could stop him, he blurted out: "Hey, stupid. You want to help? Grab the end of that goddamn litter. There's people bleeding to death in the belly of that chopper while we're sitting here with our heels locked."

"Who said that?" said the lieutenant, his eyes darting around the crammed room to see who had dared to be so insubordinate. Rather than answering, Kelley shoved past him toward the helicopter landing pad. Pawlak was first to follow Kelley, then the other medics broke rank and followed him out to the landing pad. "We unloaded the helicopter," said Kelley, "and left him standing there, like an idiot."

After Kelley's blatant disobedience, the lieutenant had it out for him. Disobeying an order meant Kelley could be court-martialed: tried before a military court, and sentenced if found guilty. But the lieutenant didn't dare try that because the nurses and medics had witnessed what had happened and they'd back Kelley. He'd been in the right.

After a month, the incoming casualties from the Tet Offensive slowed, and the hospital went back to its usual shifts: twelve hours on, twelve hours off. At the end of their long shift—it didn't matter if it was 6:00 p.m. or 6:00 a.m.—people would head to the area behind the hospital. Along with doctors, nurses, and medics, Kelley would sit in a big circle out in the sand, get stoned, and swap stories. People would bring their state-of-the-art reel-to-reel tape recorders and hook up speakers. Music was censored—they weren't allowed to play Bob Dylan, the Byrds, or Joan Baez. Any kind of folk music or rock and roll was out. Any references to drugs, sex, or defiance of authority were out. Instead they mostly listened to rhythm and blues (R&B), busting out cool dance moves and lip-synching along.

R&B was just fine with Kelley. He loved the music so much that two other medics, Stringer and the Walrus, pulled him to his feet and even got him to mouth the words. Stringer was the most aggressive medic Kelley knew: quick to anger, lightning-fast to resort to violence, but the music mellowed him out. He and the Walrus—named for his handlebar mustache—taught Kelley the moves to the Mashed Potato, the Boogaloo, and the Funky Chicken, and put him right in the middle. "You got two black guys and a skinny white kid," said Kelley. "They called us the Oreos." Pawlak cheered them on from the circle.

Sometimes, lying in their bunks long after their shift had ended, talk would turn serious between Pawlak and Kelley. They'd have long discussions about life, and what they would and wouldn't do to survive. One night Pawlak asked Kelley a direct question. "You know, we're close," said Pawlak. "But what if we get down to the last bullet, the last C ration, the last chance, what is going to happen?"

Kelley had thought hard about surviving—or dying—in Vietnam. He had a repetitive drumbeat in his head: *you are going to die here*. "It's a real subtle change that happens inside of you," said Kelley later. "Your morality becomes compromised the instant you put yourself above anyone else. As you begin kicking these things around in your head, or with someone else, you trigger things, and you realize you are just not going to go down."

"Don't turn your back on me," he said to Pawlak. He was serious. But inside, his feelings were roiling. As a medic, he was willing to take any kind of risk in order to save a life. "My patients were worth dying for," he said. And he'd do almost anything for Pawlak. *Almost.*

The lieutenant kept up his relentless pursuit of Kelley. One day he walked in on Kelley working with a heavily bleeding patient in the ER. To stop the blood loss, Kelley had pinched off an artery using a hemostat, something he wasn't officially rated to use. The lieutenant saw his chance and served him with a court-martial. The doctors and nurses sprang to his defense, and the court-martial was dropped.

One of the field medics who brought patients in, Ric Painter, offered to train Kelley as a medic on a Dust Off helicopter in the 50th Medical Detachment. Kelley jumped at the chance to leave the hospital.

Kelley was assigned to a helicopter piloted by Major Jones, a tough, seasoned pilot. He drank like a fish, was highly opinionated, and was a fearless helicopter pilot. He had a capable, quiet copilot. The crew chief, Red, a hulking redheaded guy from Tennessee, maintained the helicopter and served as the door gunner during flights.

At first Painter flew with Kelley in the helicopter, known as a "medevac" ship, short for medical evacuation. Painter gave Kelly a quick, intense crash course in his new job. "He taught me how to prepare when I'm on the radio talking to the ground medic," said Kelley. "I'm getting out what I need and hanging it on the poles. Getting stuff ready. Opening up packages of bandages and getting them ready to go, because I know which ones I'm going to need."

Kelley was in awe of Painter's skill as he watched him care for the injured men during the flight. "He could do an appendectomy with a teaspoon in the back of a roller coaster," said Kelley. Painter taught Kelley how to "roll and stuff" a sucking chest wound. "You roll them on the bad lung, stuff it full of crap. Cut off as much air as possible going into the hole. Hold him—prop him in place, with whatever you got."

After a couple of weeks, Painter knew he could trust Kelley to handle the job alone. One of the first things Kelley did was spray-paint over the Red Cross on his helicopter. "I got rid of it," Kelley said. It was supposed to signal to the enemy that the crew carried only light weapons to defend themselves. For humanitarian reasons, they should be left alone. But this was a guerrilla war, and the usual rules didn't apply. "It's a target," said Kelley. "There's a big red cross on the bottom of the helicopter, and just above it there are one hundred fifty gallons of fuel." Jones didn't make Kelley change it back. He'd been fired on too many times himself.

Now life-and-death decisions were up to Kelley. Many of the patients were losing blood fast from their wounds and had to have intravenous blood or plasma to stay alive. Kelley would do a "cut down," using his scalpel to cut quickly and firmly into the flesh at the wrist or ankle to locate the vein—without cutting through it—to insert the needle. "I could do a cut down in the middle of a firefight," said Kelley.

Members of a US helicopter crew race to be rescued after being shot down, 1967. The pilot made an emergency landing in a grassy area covered with two feet of water.

"Blew everybody away. I just totally focused just on it. Three-quarters of a square inch of skin, man; looking for that vein.

"You can't imagine what the interior of sixteen or eighteen cubic feet is like with all of these people screaming, and yelling, and talking, and howling," said Kelley. "Not to mention the radio squealing. And bullets flying. And explosions going up. You just can't imagine the chaos that goes through your head. And it requires immense concentration, and effort, to focus on what your job is."

With more than one operation going on at times, someone had to decide which wounded to pick up first, and if an area was secure enough to get in and get out. At some point in the approach, Jones would tell Kelley he was now responsible for commanding the helicopter. "Oh no, no, no, don't put that on me, man," Kelley said. But that was the way Jones ran his ship.

Aluminum shipping caskets containing bodies are stacked outside the US Army Mortuary facility at Tan Sun Nhut Airbase near Saigon, 1969. With so many deaths occurring each week, the priority was transferring the bodies back to the United States as quickly as possible. To avoid demoralizing troops, flights carrying the containers to America took place at night.

And there were the hard economics of warfare to consider. "That medevac ship is much more valuable than people," said Kelley. If the helicopter got shot down, many men would not be able to be medevacked out. "My job was to ascertain if the casualty warranted the risk," said Kelley. "We wore these big helmets with these big speakers and mikes in there." He could talk with the crew chief, the pilot, and the copilot. "Ideally I'm talking to the medic on the ground, or I'm talking to the communications guy over the radio."

Kelley's decision—go in or fly on—had to be made fast. Injured men below desperately needed medical care. But if he took too great a risk, the helicopter could be shot down, plunging him and the rest of the crew to their deaths. It was horrific to choose between the lives of the men in the helicopter and the wounded on the ground. But Major Jones was unyielding. What he said went.

In August they received an urgent call to pick up a wounded sergeant. He had two sucking chest wounds and an abdominal wound. "He was real important to them," said Kelley. "He was the most experienced guy." As always, Jones handed command of the helicopter over to Kelley.

It was a tough call. There were still enemies on the ground, making it a hot LZ. But Kelley decided it was worth getting the sergeant. "Batten down your ship, Red," said Kelley, "get your shit together, we're going in." Once they landed, it quickly became clear the infantry were too busy just trying to survive to bring the wounded man to the helicopter. Kelley yanked off his helmet, grabbed his shotgun, and went out to pick up the sergeant.

He almost made it back to the chopper with the wounded man cradled in his arms. "As I carried him to the helicopter," said Kelley, "he took a slug right in the head. Blew his brains all over me." Shrapnel hit Kelley in the back and legs, and the force of the blast slammed him against the helicopter. Dazed and injured, he slumped to his knees. Red managed to hoist him on board, and they took off. Kelley was now the wounded pickup.

It took three hours to get all the shrapnel out of Kelley's back and legs. The next day he was back at work, bandaged, bruised, and barely able to walk. He wasn't going to lie around in a hospital bed if he could help it.

But the more pickups he did, the tougher the job got. "I got tired of making those decisions," Kelley said. "I failed a bunch of times. That's the absolute truth. I missed some things. And people died."

Kelley began to dread the radio calls that came in requesting a Dust Off. "I just got to where I couldn't handle it anymore. I couldn't walk to the helicopter. My feet wouldn't work." Jones and Red would stand on either side of him and take him by the elbows. "Yeah, well," they'd say, cajoling him as they walked him toward the helicopter. "We're going now."

Once they were airborne, Kelley was able to function. But back on the ground, he was dogged by nightmares filled with the faces of the men who died. He couldn't shake the feeling he was personally responsible for not saving them.

With so much death and dying in Vietnam, Kelley's conviction that he would die in Vietnam grew until it hung over him like an inevitable, inescapable destiny. He was no longer convinced he would be willing to do *anything* to survive, or that he even had a right to live. Why should he still be alive when so many others weren't, men he should have been able to help?

One night, racked by exhaustion and guilt, he picked up his .45 and put the barrel in his mouth. He'd just blow his brains out and get it over with. His mind swung wildly back and forth. *Do it. No, put the gun down.* A voice in his head came into focus: *You have your whole life ahead of you. You are going to live through this.* He put the gun down.

It was an endless mental turmoil that went on whenever he wasn't working. Night after night, Kelley picked up his gun and considered shooting himself. Days, he was frog-marched out to the helicopter and did his job. Finally he realized he needed to get out, and he didn't want to do it by committing suicide. He asked for a transfer back to his old unit.

Even back at the hospital, Kelley was still on edge. His old nemesis, the lieutenant, was watching him like a hawk, waiting for him to mess up. One day, Kelley was talking with a buddy of his who was getting ready to leave Vietnam. Just as Kelley's friend opened his footlocker, the lieutenant walked into the room.

Kelley's buddy flashed him a hand signal indicating he had drugs in his locker.

There was a code of honor among the dope-smoking buddies: if someone was "holding," the person closest to the officer would create a diversion so the drugs could be tossed away. Kelley stepped in front of the lieutenant and started an argument. It quickly escalated, and the animosity between the two men exploded. Kelley slugged the lieutenant, and for good measure, hit him a second time. It was a stupid, costly thing to do, but Kelley didn't hesitate to cover for his buddy. "We had a deal," said Kelley. "We were brothers. And the deal is, I take the heat and he goes home."

Kelley wasn't going to be able to get out of this one. He was sentenced to six months in Long Binh Jail. After his sentence was pronounced, his lawyer leaned over and whispered to him, "I'll have you out in two to three weeks."

Kelley was assigned to his cell twelve hours a day, and taken out for twelve-hour work shifts, building fortifications and doing other heavy manual labor. To Kelley's immense relief, his lawyer somehow managed to get him out of jail in three weeks, as he'd promised.

Sent back to the hospital, Kelley had only a few weeks left in country. He and his buddy Stringer were leaving the same day, and they threw a huge party. "We were cooking purloined steaks and lobster we stole from the officer's club and the mess hall," said Kelley.

On Christmas Day, totally hungover from too many drugs and too much sun, Kelley and Stringer shipped out on the same plane. Kelley had been in Vietnam for exactly one year. He was alive, but he barely cared. He felt bone-weary and soulless.

Still in uniform, the men arrived at the Seattle airport. As the men walked through the terminal, a young woman came toward them, angrily shouting that they were baby killers. As she got close to Kelley and Stringer, she spit on Stringer.

Kelley was instantly alarmed. They were just hours out of Vietnam, where life-and-death decisions were made with swift finality, and no one messed with Stringer. But two big, burly soldiers right behind them grabbed Stringer's arms before he could even react, and forced him to keep moving.

Outside the terminal, they went separate ways. It took a long time before the adrenaline quit coursing through Kelley.

President Johnson listens to an audiotape sent from Vietnam by Captain Charles Robb, his son-in-law, 1968.

AMERICA:
PRESIDENT AND COMMANDER IN CHIEF

LYNDON B. JOHNSON
MARCH 1968–DECEMBER 1968

"The blow to morale was more of our own doing than anything the enemy had accomplished with its army. We were defeating ourselves."

ON THE AFTERNOON of March 31, 1968, Johnson was in his bedroom preparing for a live televised speech. An advisor was with him, putting the final touches on the dramatic ending the president had recently come up with. Johnson had told almost no one what he'd decided, and his advisor was eager to get the wording just right. Johnson paced the floor, talking on the phone. He called in his new secretary of defense, Clark Clifford, recently appointed to replace Robert McNamara. Johnson shocked Clifford when he told him how the speech would end. "I've made up my mind," Johnson said. "I'm actually going to do it."

In the Oval Office, tarps were being spread out on the floor to protect the rug. Heavy television cameras and audio equipment were set up, and the operators quietly waited. A few minutes before it was time to give his talk, President Johnson took his place at his desk.

Cameras rolled. "Tonight I want to speak to you of peace in Vietnam and Southeast Asia," Johnson began. He acknowledged the high price exacted by the war in human death and suffering, and assured listeners he was eager to negotiate a settlement. He defended the difficult choices he had made in Vietnam to stop a Communist takeover and praised the troops who'd done the fighting.

"I believe that a peaceful Asia is far nearer to reality because of what America has done in Vietnam," he said. "I believe that the men who endure the dangers of battle—fighting there for us tonight—are helping the entire world avoid far greater conflicts, far wider wars, far more destruction, than this one."

But the brutal truth was that he'd become mired more and more deeply in an unending, bloody conflict. Since sending in the Marines three years earlier, Johnson had been unable to bomb, fight, or negotiate his way to victory in Vietnam. At home, the war had created a sharp, angry division between the "hawks" who supported the war effort and the "doves" who wanted peace. From Tet onward, public confidence in Johnson had eroded until it was at an all-time low.

Everyone—including Johnson—had assumed he would seek a second full term as president, but he knew now his chances of reelection were bleak. As millions of Americans watched, he concluded his speech. "I shall not seek, and I will not accept, the nomination of my party for another term as your president."

Shortly after Johnson's speech, the North Vietnamese agreed to meet with the United States in Paris, France, for preliminary negotiations to end the war. A few months later, the South Vietnamese and the Viet Cong were invited to join the talks, now known as the Paris Peace Accords. But animosity ran high between the different factions. By the end of the year, the only issue they had resolved was the shape of the conference table where they would all sit for the talks.

The war had cost Johnson a chance of another term as president. He would not be able to go any further with his Great Society policies to eliminate poverty and social injustice. Despite the huge divide now between Johnson and King, it was a profound loss shared by the two men.

Johnson was convinced the battlefield was not where he had been unable to win the war. It was at home, with the country convulsing in turmoil and protest. Instead of Johnson having the country behind him, America was more divided than it had been since the Civil War.

Antiwar demonstrators surround a statue honoring a Union Civil War general in Chicago, 1968.
They were protesting police actions during the Democratic National Convention.

Richard Nixon (right) *confers with President Johnson in the Oval Office on the day Nixon was inaugurated, 1969.*

AMERICA:
PRESIDENT AND COMMANDER IN CHIEF

RICHARD M. NIXON
JANUARY 1969

"I can assure you, the humiliation of a defeat is absolutely unacceptable to my country."

AMERICANS ELECTED A new president, Richard Nixon, who had campaigned on a promise to bring "an honorable end to the war in Vietnam." On January 20, 1968, he and his family moved into the White House.

Nixon slept terribly that first night. Early in the morning he gave up and headed for the shower. While he was shaving, he remembered a few months earlier, President Johnson had shown him the hidden safe where he stashed top secret documents. Curious, Nixon opened the safe and found only one thin folder inside. It was yesterday's Vietnam Situation Report, left behind from Johnson's last day as president. Nixon carefully thumbed through it. On the final page was a list of casualties. In just over the twelve months of Johnson's last year in office, January 1, 1968, to January 18, 1969, 14,958 Americans had been killed and 95,798 wounded. The numbers were staggering, a visceral reminder of the war's tragic cost.

Nixon shoved the folder back in and locked the safe. The war was no longer Johnson's war. Nixon was the new commander in chief, and it was *his* war now, to win or lose.

He had already come up with a surefire winning strategy, one that required not just secrecy but lies. That didn't bother Nixon. "If you can't lie," he'd once said to a friend, "you'll never go anywhere."

While he was campaigning, Nixon had revealed his tactic to his chief of staff, H. R. Haldeman. After a long day of speech writing, the two men had taken a walk along a foggy beach. "I call it the Madman Theory," Nixon confided. "I want the North Vietnamese to believe I've reached the point where I might do *anything* to stop the war. We'll just slip the word to them that, 'for God's sake, you know Nixon is obsessed about Communism. We can't restrain him when he's angry—and he has his hand on the nuclear button'—and Ho Chi Minh himself will be in Paris in two days begging for peace."

Now that he'd been elected president, he could put his plan into action.

President Nixon walks with his chief of staff, H. R. Haldeman, to a cabinet meeting, 1969.

Jan Scruggs on his second day in Vietnam, 1969.

VIETNAM: INFANTRYMAN

JAN SCRUGGS
IN COUNTRY APRIL 1969—APRIL 1970

"It was just a screwed-up thing. A random incident in a war. I mean, twelve people? Is that a lot of people? To us, that was a lot of people. These were all of our best friends. They were all dead. They were just all dead."

IN JAN SCRUGGS'S conservative family, he'd been taught it was his duty as a citizen to serve in the armed forces. He felt prepared for the military: He'd spent a lot of time as a teenager hunting and fishing in the woods, and competing in rifle competitions near his home in rural Maryland. He had avidly watched war movies, such as *In Harm's Way* and *The Red Badge of Courage*. Like his heroes in the films, he was ready to have his endurance and courage tested.

As soon as he graduated from high school in 1968, Scruggs signed up for the army and was sent to Fort Bragg, North Carolina. At the end of basic training, he was assigned his specialty: "Indirect fire crewman." He knew that meant he'd be sent to Vietnam, as a member of a mortar squad. Scruggs was ready for the challenge. "I got what I wanted," he said.

On April 15, 1969, Scruggs flew to Vietnam and joined the US Army 199th Light

Infantry Brigade. Stationed eight miles outside of Saigon, the 199th's job was to help defend Saigon against Viet Cong attack. Scruggs spent most of his time at the base. Days were long, repetitive, and boring. They'd drill occasionally and keep their equipment clean and operational. But mostly, they waited. When the ground troops needed support, Scruggs and the other mortarmen would be brought in with their 81mm mortars. He was glad his unit didn't carry out "search and destroy" missions. "I wouldn't have wanted to set fires to houses," he said, "do what those guys did."

To relieve the tedium, Scruggs began smoking marijuana. He was very cautious about when he smoked. Just before he'd arrived in Vietnam, there'd been a tragic accident in his platoon, one that everyone was still reeling from. "The guys were smoking pot and drinking beer," said Scruggs, "laughing and tossing hand grenades into a river." One drunk, stoned GI fumbled a grenade and dropped it, killing himself and a couple of other guys. Whenever Scruggs was handling explosives or firearms or out on operations, he stayed stone-cold sober.

Scruggs found about 90 percent of his company had been drafted and didn't want to be in Vietnam. They weren't worried about stopping Communism. They just wanted to survive their year in Vietnam. News from home about the continuous antiwar protests didn't help company morale. A fog of depression had settled over everyone. It was nearly impossible to fight for something you didn't believe in, for a country that didn't believe in you.

Sometimes Scruggs would go along on one of the helicopter rides to a nearby village to provide sanitation measures and simple medical care. One day Scruggs and a medic flew polio vaccines out to a friendly village. The village, like many in Vietnam, had high rates of polio, a disease that caused muscle weakness, even paralysis. The vaccine was explained to the village chief and his wife. After careful consideration, the chief decided everyone should be vaccinated. One by one, adults and children stepped forward for vaccination.

The Americans left feeling good about what they had done. A few days later, word reached them about what happened after they left. "The Viet Cong brought the village chief and his wife into the middle of the village," said Scruggs, "and blew them

An ironic sign in a war zone at a US defensive position seven miles northeast of Saigon, 1969.

up to retaliate for them accepting the vaccine." It was a typical Viet Cong action, making it dangerous for villagers to have anything to do with the Americans, even accepting life-saving medical care. No matter who the villagers sided with, they risked terrible reprisals from the other side. It sickened Scruggs that one of the life-giving things he'd done had turned into a disaster.

On May 27, Scruggs's unit was taken to an area near the village of Xuan Loc, east of Saigon. The 11th Armored Cavalry was there, taking heavy losses. This was a ground operation, and Scruggs was carrying his M16 rifle through the dense jungle foliage. He hadn't been in heavy combat before, and like many of the others, he was scared, not sure what to expect or how he would behave in combat. Would he freeze with fear? Shoot too early or too late?

Someone saw a North Vietnamese soldier, took a shot at him, and missed. They radioed their commanding officer and asked what he wanted them to do.

The commanding officer told them to go after the NVA soldier. Nineteen-year-old Sergeant Claude Van Andel, experienced in the jungle, volunteered to "walk point" and took the lead position of the foot patrol. It was a relief to Scruggs—he liked Van Andel, and trusted his judgment.

Van Andel set out, with Scruggs about one hundred yards behind him. Suddenly Scruggs heard the blast of a claymore mine. Van Andel took the full explosion of the blast and was killed. Shooting erupted from all sides, and Scruggs threw himself down on the ground. The Americans had been drawn into an ambush. In the brief, furious fight that followed, another man was killed and at least ten more wounded. Scruggs realized they were fighting troops with excellent training. "They were good marksmen," Scruggs said. "They knew how to hold their fire. They were well managed. This was the deep, dark jungle. We were walking into their home. And they knew exactly what to do in order to get the upper hand. Which was just wait for us. They could hear us coming about a mile away."

After the battle, Scruggs struggled to make sense of what had happened. One minute Van Andel was alive, the next, he was dead. Scruggs helped load him into a body bag and carry it over to where the helicopter could retrieve his body. It wasn't much, but it was all he could do to show his respect.

That evening, Scruggs's company linked up with another company, as well as some American tanks and armored personnel carriers. Now they had 250 or 300 guys. "We had all these tanks," said Scruggs, "and we had artillery we could call in around us because we thought maybe we would have more action in the next day." Scruggs was relieved. Now there would be safety in numbers, with equipment to back them up.

The armored personnel carrier drivers were there to take them farther into the jungle and warned them about the intense action they'd been experiencing. They were being constantly ambushed and had been firing a thousand or more rounds a day. One bluntly told Scruggs, "I don't know how any of us are going to make it back." Tomorrow they would be in more danger, not less.

After a night of fitful sleep on the ground, Scruggs woke up with an eerie premonition he was going to be shot in the back. He took his rain poncho and folded it over and over again until it was only about eight inches wide and a foot long. He jammed it under his pistol belt to cover the small of his back. "It protected me from my waist down over my rear end," he said. "It made a thick wad of plastic."

Now that he'd been in an ambush and seen men injured and killed, he was also ruthlessly ready to fight. "Mentally I was completely prepared to fire my weapon and to destroy any enemy that was anywhere near me," he said.

Using tanks and armored personnel carriers, troops move into the jungle near the Cambodian border to search for a suspected Viet Cong base camp, 1970.

The armored personnel carriers dropped everyone off near an old rubber plantation. Divided into two groups, they moved as quietly as they could through the plantation and into the surrounding jungle in single-file lines, searching for the North Vietnamese. Tension built as they found fresh footprints and spent bullets on the ground. The NVA was unnervingly close.

They didn't have to wait long. The attack came fast and furious, overwhelming the American troops. Scruggs threw himself down on his belly and fired blindly into the dense jungle foliage. He could hear the American tanks firing over the nearby explosions of grenades, rocket-propelled grenades, and small-arms fire. "There was a lot of confusion, chaos," said Scruggs. "The enemy was in a base camp, and we killed quite a few of them there. But there were also other little bands of enemy soldiers who went all along the line of American soldiers, picking us off."

Scruggs and two other infantrymen were pinned down about fifty feet from a North Vietnamese machine-gun emplacement. But that didn't explain where all the firepower was coming from. Finally he figured it out. "They were up in the trees, throwing grenades down on us," Scruggs said. "They had us targeted, basically."

He sprinted for cover behind a nearby tree. A few seconds later a grenade exploded where he'd been lying, sending up a shower of plants and dirt, leaving a crater three feet wide.

Another grenade landed nearby, and shrapnel tore into him in a dozen places. Blood from his injuries quickly blossomed on his uniform. He noticed his right arm was sticking out at a weird angle. He tried to move it. No response. He shoved his left hand into his armpit and pulled it back out. His cupped hand was full of his warm, sticky blood, and more was quickly pumping out.

Scruggs repeated the Lord's Prayer to himself, but it brought him no comfort. *I'm going to be dead within minutes in this little nothing battle in Vietnam that's not going to change the course of the war*, he thought. The valiant, critical battles of World War II flashed through his mind. *This is not like Normandy, or Stalingrad*, he thought. *This is just a skirmish.* Scruggs felt furious he was going to bleed to death next to a tree in Vietnam.

Armed with a shotgun, a soldier provides cover for a buddy crawling to safety after their tank was hit by armor-piercing grenades, 1969.

Through the noise of explosions, tank fire, and shouting and screaming men, Scruggs thought he heard someone yelling his name. "There was more shooting, and then they came and got me," Scruggs said. Three men belly-crawled to him, despite sniper fire. Keeping flat to the ground, they pushed a poncho under Scruggs as a stretcher, then dragged him to safety.

A chunk of shrapnel the size of a golf ball had lodged in the poncho in the middle of his lower back. Without the layers of plastic protecting him, the shrapnel would have severed his spine. The next two months Scruggs spent in a bed in the hospital.

Scruggs was awarded a Purple Heart and sent back to his company. Once again his time was mostly spent waiting, drilling, and taking care of his equipment. He played cards, listened to the American Forces Vietnam Network (AFVN), and read the magazines that passed hand to hand. One issue, *Life* magazine's "The Faces of

Scruggs waits his turn while PFC Wright takes his cold-water shower at Fire Support Base Nancy in Xuan Loc, Vietnam, 1969. When the Charlie Company truck caught fire in a mortar explosion on January 21, 1970, Wright quickly grabbed a fire extinguisher, ran to the truck, and sprayed the burning ammo to put out the fire.

the American Dead in Vietnam: One Week's Toll," with photographs of the 242 men killed the week of May 28 through June 3, 1969, deeply upset him. In the layout, the faces of the men with their names below filled the double-page spreads like a high-school yearbook. But their promise of a bright future was gone.

Given the policies of the military, Scruggs was surprised when the army announced there would be a screening of the popular antiwar movie *Alice's Restaurant*. Scruggs joined about 300 other guys to watch the folk singer Arlo Guthrie defy attempts by the government to draft him. "When Arlo Guthrie gave the finger to the army sergeant, everyone started applauding except for the career guys," said Scruggs. "It was funny. I could not believe the army would show it. The entire audience was in the middle of the war taking casualties every day." It seemed incongruous that so many drafted men would be cheering on the defiant Guthrie, but it was GI humor at its best, a dark way of expressing anger without getting in trouble.

Scruggs found the war deeply demoralizing. "The enemy was clearly not being defeated," said Scruggs, despite American troops having been on the ground for five years. "I could not see how the South Vietnamese could win once we left, given the skill level of the North Vietnamese—and their determination."

On the morning of January 21, 1970, Scruggs was in one of the mortar pits getting ready to clean his gun when a truck loaded with unused 81mm mortars pulled in to a nearby pit. The mortar platoon of Charlie Company had been out providing support to the infantry. With the operation over, the exhausted men had put the unused mortar shells back into the cases, stacked them in the truck, and driven back to the base. They were eager to get the truck unloaded, and get breakfast, a hot shower, and some sleep.

But out in the field, someone had missed a critically important step. Some of the mortar safety pins, which kept the priming mechanism from allowing the round to detonate on impact, had not been replaced.

The twelve men of the platoon pitched in to unload the truck. Suddenly there was an earthshaking blast as one of the mortars exploded. Scruggs ran to the mortar pit and was first to arrive. The men torn apart by the blast were all his friends, his combat

A medic performs mouth-to-mouth resuscitation in a desperate attempt to save the life of a seriously wounded fellow medic, 1969. The injured medic later died of his injuries.

brothers. "There were brains, arms, legs, all mixed together. It was like you would imagine hell. Some of them were on fire, some were moaning. . . . " said Scruggs. "Billy Moore, his brains were lying out of his head." Scruggs screamed for a medic. From all over the base, others were already coming at a run. Scruggs dropped to his knees next to John Kroeger and desperately tried to bandage a big hole right in the middle of his head. Someone told Scruggs to stop. It was no use.

The truck burst into flame. "It had hundreds of mortar rounds that would have blown up everything within hundreds of yards," said Scruggs. "But we didn't care. Everybody went to the truck and got their fire extinguishers and put it out."

Just outside the mortar pit, Scruggs saw John Pies, a rifleman with his company who'd been walking by. He was flat on the ground, completely still, not even breathing. He had no wounds anywhere. "No one could tell what had happened to him," said Scruggs. "We were trying to get him breathing again." But they had to give up and admit Pies was beyond help. The concussive blast had killed him outright.

Scruggs was devastated. The explosion and horrific result played and replayed in his mind. "I was ready for combat," Scruggs said, "but I wasn't ready to see people die. I didn't know how bad that was, and what my reaction would be. It was a very difficult thing to deal with."

A few months later, Scruggs's year in Vietnam was up. He'd been in the army for nineteen months and had less than five months of service left to fulfill his two-year military commitment. According to army policy, anyone who had served a full year in Vietnam and had five months or less left in their two-year military commitment would receive an immediate discharge as soon as they were back in the United States.

By the time Scruggs was ready to leave Vietnam, he was bitter and disillusioned. The men in his company had done what the country had asked of them, but the cost was staggering. Half the men in his company had been killed or wounded. Just what had they accomplished? As far as he was concerned, it had been a yearlong nightmare.

Scruggs was discharged the same day he deplaned from Vietnam in Oakland, California. He was given a briefcase and his honorable discharge papers, and fed a steak dinner. A bus took him and others fresh from Vietnam to the San Francisco airport, and they were told to find their own flights home. With a quick handshake, they were informed, "You are now no longer soldiers. You're military veterans."

President Nixon during a press conference, 1969. Most of the questions reporters asked concerned the war.

AMERICA:
PRESIDENT AND COMMANDER IN CHIEF

RICHARD M. NIXON
FEBRUARY 1969–JUNE 1969

"I will not be the first president of
the United States to lose a war."

AFTER NIXON'S FIRST few weeks in office, increasingly war-weary Americans wanted to see his plan for Vietnam. So did the Communists in North Vietnam. They slipped into South Vietnam in February 1969 and mounted several devastating attacks. "It was a deliberate test," said Nixon, "clearly designed to take the measure of me and my administration at the outset." The Communist assults were also intended to make a statement about the ongoing Paris Peace Accords: the North Vietnamese would not be pushed around.

Members of the press repeatedly asked Nixon, what was he going to do now? His immediate instinct was to retaliate against the North Vietnamese, but he held back. He didn't want the Communists to think they could manipulate him. Instead, he would strike later, on his own terms.

Sunday, March 16, Nixon decided it was time to put his Madman Theory, conceived the previous fall, into action. Nixon's day was recorded in the official White House Daily Diary, a scrupulously accurate record of what he did and when, and whom he did it with. He began his Sunday with a twelve-minute phone call to his national security advisor, Henry Kissinger, a staunch believer in the Madman Theory. Breakfast with three reporters followed. Nixon and his wife, Pat, attended the White House church services with 125 guests, their names carefully listed in Appendix A in the Daily Diary.

After lunch and several more phone calls, the president went to his office at 4:30 p.m., where his top military advisors joined him. The meeting was so secret, it was not even recorded in the Daily Diary. "Gentlemen," Nixon said to the gathered men, "we have reached the point where a decision is required: to bomb or not to bomb."

It wasn't North Vietnam Nixon was talking about. He was after the North Vietnamese troops just across the border in Cambodia that were moving into Vietnam, attacking, and running back into Cambodia to hide in the jungle. Nixon wanted to destroy their camps. It wouldn't be the first time American planes had dropped their payload on Cambodia. President Johnson had secretly ordered more than two thousand bombing runs over Cambodia during his presidency. But Nixon was planning a significant escalation in the air attacks. Even though Cambodia was a neutral nation, to him the end justified the means.

Nixon was convinced he could force concessions from the Communists in the Paris peace talks with heavy bombing in Cambodia. The North Vietnamese would see what happened when he unleashed some of his firepower, but they wouldn't be able to protest. After all, they weren't supposed to be in Cambodia either. The raids would show the Communists just how irrational and volatile he was. "It would be a signal," agreed Kissinger, "that things may get out of hand."

Nixon ordered bombing for the next day. To provide an alibi, he ordered air strikes right up to the edge of the Vietnam-Cambodia border, starting twelve hours before they would cross into Cambodia. If the press got wind of the Cambodian sorties, he could claim American planes had strayed accidentally over the border.

That evening Nixon escorted Pat to her surprise birthday party in the State Dining Room. In the White House, life went on. In Cambodia, death and destruction were about to fall from the skies.

The first reports that air strikes were under way came in on Monday. By Tuesday morning, there was more detailed news: forty-eight B-52 bombers from the American Air Force base in Guam had set off for Vietnam, been told in midflight to change their flight paths, and dropped their payloads over Cambodia. The military report showed the bombing was a "great success," hitting not only primary targets, but more secondary targets than expected. Nixon and Kissinger were both excited to see their plan in action.

But the North Vietnamese refused to make any concessions. Nixon increased the pressure on the Communists by expanding the Cambodian air strikes into Operation Menu, a staggering series of heavy, repeated carpet-bombings. To ensure secrecy held up, Nixon had the Air Force falsify reports on the bombing runs to look as if they took place over South Vietnam. Actual reports were carefully sent outside normal channels directly to Nixon, Kissinger, and a small handful of other officials.

In June, Nixon publicly made a major shift in his strategy and announced a new policy, called Vietnamization. The American military would substantially increase their equipping and training of South Vietnamese forces so the ARVN could take full responsibility for fighting the war themselves. Nixon promised he would begin a drawdown of American troops. Vietnamization would show the North Vietnamese he was serious about working out a diplomatic solution, and at the same time assure Americans the war would soon be over. He didn't reveal his clandestine bombing of Cambodia.

Protestors didn't buy Nixon's new policy for peace. There were still more than half a million US troops in Vietnam, and weekly death tolls continued to mount. Antiwar activists wanted the Unites States out of Vietnam, honor or no honor. Within weeks they began organizing for a massive, all-out demonstration to be held in the fall: the Moratorium to End the War in Vietnam.

Overleaf: *In a thick fog, Marines search for a Viet Cong weapons cache after heavy bombing by US planes, 1969.*

David Oshiro at Army Airborne School at Fort Benning, Georgia, 1969.

VIETNAM: GREEN BERET

DAVID OSHIRO
IN COUNTRY MAY 1969—MAY 1970

"I was getting it from both sides. It made me real paranoid. I didn't know who to trust."

DAVID OSHIRO WAS in the eleventh grade when his brother Robert came home on leave from Vietnam. Oshiro was awestruck when he saw Robert. On his military coat were sergeant stripes, paratrooper "jump wings," and a ranger patch. He wore a dark green beret, precisely folded over to the right. It was 1966, and Robert was a member of the elite Special Forces of the army, known as the Green Berets for their distinctive headgear. "It was magical, exciting, and wonderful," said Oshiro.

The eighth of ten kids, Oshiro had grown up in a small town in Hawaii. Stretching in every direction were huge fields of sugarcane. Oshiro was free to run around the neighborhood with packs of other kids, play in the streams, and roam the fields. He never had to wear shoes, not even to school. Instead of standard English, everyone spoke Hawaiian Pidgin, a language mash-up created by Hawaiians and early Chinese, Filipino, Japanese, and American immigrants. One by one, Oshiro's three older brothers had left Hawaii to join the military and were sent to Vietnam.

After graduating from high school, Oshiro received his draft notice. Robert urged his brother to enlist in the army for three years, rather than be drafted for two. That

Oshiro (front row, middle) *with his parents and four of his siblings, 1959.*

way he could choose his own MOS—Military Occupational Specialty. He could pick something safe, and stay out of combat in Vietnam. Oshiro figured his brother knew what he was talking about. He signed on for three years and was sent for basic training to Fort Ord, California. It was the first time he'd ever been off the Hawaiian Islands. He had to quickly learn to speak standard mainland English to be understood.

Basic training was exhausting and intimidating, but more troubling were the complex, identity-shaking challenges for Oshiro and other Asian Americans. Sometimes the dummies for bayonet practice had "slant eyes" drawn on them, and enlistees would be ordered to chant as they stabbed the bayonet into the body, "Kill, kill." Who were they supposed to kill? "Luke the Gook" and "Link the Chink."

It became personal for Oshiro when a sergeant asked him and several other Asian Americans to wear loose black cotton shirts and pants like the Viet Cong wore, to show the other recruits what the enemy looked like. Oshiro was horrified by the thought of being asked to portray the men they were being trained to fight, and wouldn't comply. Because it was a request and not an order, he didn't face disciplinary action for his refusal.

Oshiro wanted to be a paratrooper like his brother Robert. He signed up for the Army Airborne School, known as "Jump School," and learned to parachute from planes. He went on to train as a parachute rigger and was sent to Panama. In a huge

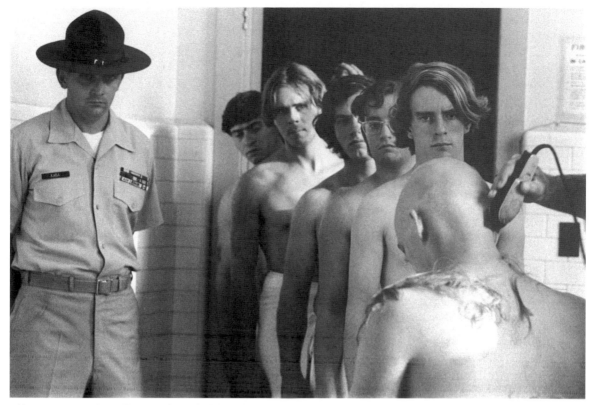

Young Marine trainees line up to have their hair shorn at training camp in Parris Island, South Carolina, 1971.

room filled with long tables, he and the other riggers each stood at a long table, folding the billowing nylon canopy of each parachute, packing it carefully so the suspension lines couldn't tangle. Oshiro was acutely aware that other men's lives depended on his thoroughness. Every day he packed forty parachutes, each time with the same meticulous care. "Of course," he said, "we had to jump our own packed chutes once a month, chosen by the inspecting sergeant. Sometimes twice a month."

After six months of packing parachutes, Oshiro was tired of the long, repetitive days. He needed to be challenged. *That's it*, he said to himself. *I'm going to go to Vietnam.*

Oshiro stepped all the way in: he wanted the training and prestige that went with being a Green Beret. He wanted to test himself, to see if he could measure up to their standards. It was tough, as he knew it would be. The training was more challenging than boot camp, mentally and physically. Being a strong, motivated, hardened American

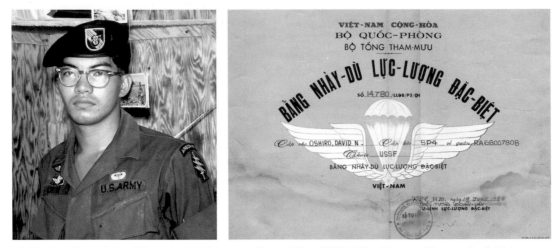

Oshiro in uniform; the certificate for his Vietnamese "Jump Wings," 1969. US soldiers could earn a South Vietnamese parachutist badge as well as American versions.

soldier was drummed into Oshiro and every member of the Special Forces until they were the elite force the army expected.

After completing Special Forces training, he was sent to Vietnam in May 1969 and assigned to the 5th Special Forces Group (Airborne). Oshiro was proud to be wearing the green beret, and ready for anything Vietnam could throw at him. "We were immortal," he said. "Being Special Forces, the beret symbolized something just a little bit more. We were like peacocks; we strutted around and did the whole thing. Just full of oats."

A few weeks after getting to Vietnam, Oshiro was sent on a routine sweep of a small island a few miles off the coast. There had been numerous reports of VC activity on the island, and the Green Berets went out with new South Vietnamese troops on a training exercise. Everyone—Vietnamese and Americans—wore tiger-striped jungle fatigues. "There is no way I'm going to put a beret on my head and go out in the field," Oshiro said. The VC always tried to kill off the best-trained American troops.

Oshiro was assigned responsibility for the radio and told he could hand it off to one of the Vietnamese they were training, as long as he kept an eye on it. "I'm putting this sucker on," Oshiro replied. "I am not giving it up to anyone." It sat heavily on his back. When he switched it on, the radio crackled and popped and was full of static. He knew, even when he was wearing fatigues, the radio alone made him an obvious target. The VC would try to knock out communications. But in uniform or not, Oshiro felt invincible.

The troops moved carefully through the heavy jungle. Suddenly they were under sniper fire. In the rapid firefight, several men were hit. A bullet whined into Oshiro's radio, ricocheted off, and plunged into his neck. Oshiro went down, the radio still on his back. Minutes later the VC were gone, leaving no trace.

As Oshiro lay on the ground with blood soaking into his uniform, he heard the reassuring *whup-whup-whup* as the medevac landed nearby. The medic spotted him and headed over. He got close, glanced at Oshiro, and said to another soldier, "Don't worry about the gook; we'll get him later," and turned and walked away.

Oshiro was furious, and terrified. He could bleed to death while they ignored him, thinking he was just a "gook." He fumbled in his shirt and grabbed his dog tags, hanging on a chain around his neck. He yanked them out and yelled at the retreating medic, "I'm an American!"

The shocked medic hurried back and evacuated him with the other Americans. At the hospital, Oshiro was rushed into surgery. The bullet had hit bone and fragmented. The doctors removed as much as they could. When Oshiro came out of anesthesia, they told him he was lucky the bullet had hit the radio first. A direct hit—just an inch or so over—would have gone right into his spine and paralyzed or killed him.

For the next three weeks, Oshiro was stuck in a bed in the 8th Field Hospital with deeply embedded tubes draining his wound. Finally they were pulled out, and he was given a choice: he could be reassigned to the American base in Okinawa, or he could stay in Vietnam. It was an easy decision for Oshiro. He'd been shot: this was personal now. He wanted to stay and fight.

Oshiro was sent to Da Nang in central Vietnam and assigned to duty as a supply sergeant. In Da Nang, the Marines from the airbase right next to them repeatedly mistook Oshiro for Vietnamese. "Hey, when did they give those Chinks berets?" he overheard one Marine say to another. It was humiliating. "I heard so many derogatory remarks," Oshiro said. He was called "gook" more times than he could even count. And this was from men he was fighting with.

The Americans had a long list of names they called the Vietnamese—"zipperheads," "slants," and "gooks" were just a few—which were constantly reinforced by the officers. "They just hammer you and hammer you and hammer you," said Oshiro. "Day and night. They dehumanized those people so badly; we never, ever called them Vietnamese. Everything else but."

It didn't stop with mistaken identification by other Americans. When Oshiro would go into town, Vietnamese would come up to him to say, "Hey, you same-same me. Why you come kill me?" It frustrated him to be accused of betraying his race. "I put my butt on the line for these people," he said. "Both sides are working against you."

Just whom could he trust? "Being Oriental, I was probably the most paranoid person around," he said. "I always carried a 9mm Browning automatic, which my brother Robert gave me. No one knew it." He kept the gun hidden, stuck in the back waistband of his pants. "I was like a cowboy; this was just part of me." At any second, with no notice, either side might decide he was the enemy. He had to be ready to defend himself.

By the time he'd been in Da Nang a few months, Oshiro's feeling of invincibility had vaporized. "I was feeling quite mortal," he said. "Not as much piss and vinegar in me anymore." He just wanted to survive and get back home.

Once he was paired up with "Big Jim" Garrison, he felt safer. "He was half white," said Oshiro, "and half Indian." It helped that he wasn't Caucasian—he had a gut-level understanding of what Oshiro was going through. Big Jim was on his second tour, and ranked above Oshiro. He was brutally tough and on edge, with instantaneous reactions. "He was just crazier than I was," Oshiro said. "We watched each other's back for nine, ten months." The two stayed alert for problems from the enemy or even other Americans.

Though officially a supply sergeant, Oshiro had a wide array of duties. He'd help Big Jim organize ammunition, weapons, and rations for the Special Forces "A team" camps deep in the jungle. After the supplies were rigged for an airlift, Oshiro and

A wounded US paratrooper receives help from two medics in a blinding rainstorm, 1969.

Big Jim would head out in the chopper to the camps. On some flights, they flew in replacement troops, both Vietnamese and American, to the camps. On flights back to Da Nang, they brought out the injured. "We had a lot of bad wounds," Oshiro said. "Leg wounds, stomach wounds." Some of the Americans Oshiro transported to the camps were brand-new, and by the time he came back a few weeks later, they'd been killed. It was deeply distressing to him that they died too quickly for their loss to even be mourned by the others. It felt like such a lonely way to die.

Many of the isolated, heavily defended camps were on hilltops in remote locations near Vietnam's western border with Cambodia and Laos where Special Forces could keep track of enemy movement. Bringing the helicopter in for a landing could be harrowing, with hidden enemy forces eager to shoot them down.

For years, the Green Berets had been working for the CIA doing covert operations. From the camps, some Green Berets made unreported incursions into Cambodia and Laos. Oshiro never knew if he crossed any borders. Secrecy was so critical, only the highest-ranking officers knew where the men were being sent. As far as Oshiro was concerned, it was all dense, dangerous jungle when they were out on recconnaisance missions known as "recon."

"We were Sneaky Petes," said Oshiro. "The mission was to go and sneak around the jungles and get intelligence. We were trying not to encounter the enemy, because most of the time when you're sneaking around the jungle on recon, you only have six or eight guys with you. And you run into a company of two hundred fifty guys. You don't want to do that."

Besides soldiers, weapons, and supplies, Oshiro and Big Jim carried highly classified information back and forth to the camps in locked bags. No ARVN soldiers were allowed in the helicopter when the bags were on board. Oshiro didn't know what was in the bags, but the CIA sent the intelligence gathered from all the remote camps to Washington, DC, for Nixon's bombing campaign in Cambodia.

On one trip, Oshiro and Big Jim took out a minigun—a six-barreled machine gun that could fire 2,000–6,000 rounds per minute. It was not an authorized weapon for the A camp, but Big Jim had somehow managed to get his hands on it.

It took longer than they thought to get the minigun set up inside the concertina wire surrounding the camp. Oshiro and Big Jim were unable to leave before dark and had to spend the night at the camp. Early the next morning, mortar rounds started coming in, hitting hard. Suddenly, Oshiro realized he could see quick, flickering movements in the trees outside the wire. The enemy was creeping up the hill toward them in an effort to overrun the camp. If they made it through the wire, the Americans would all be killed or captured. *Oh God, these guys are getting close*, thought Oshiro. The Americans with the minigun held off until the enemy was close to the wire, then opened up with the weapon, spitting out thousands of rounds per minute. "Those guys, whoever was out there—if it was the VC or NVA that were coming

A napalm strike erupts in a fireball near patrolling US troops, 1966.

up—were very surprised." The noise and firepower was overwhelming. When the dust settled, Oshiro was shocked. "It literally cut everything down," said Oshiro, "even all the trees." The enemy either had retreated or was dead.

On other missions, Oshiro was sent out with an observation ground team to track B-52 bombing strikes. "They just carpet-bombed," Oshiro said. "Just crater after crater after crater. And most times you can't even see the aircraft. We could only hear them."

One day, Oshiro watched American planes as they dropped napalm bombs only a mile away from his team. When the bombs hit the ground, the flammable napalm gel erupted in a huge, devastating fireball. Oshiro was horrified. "It was like the end of the world," he said. "It's an incredible gas smell, and you can almost feel the heat from the distance. It's just unbelievable. It's like that movie, *Apocalypse Now*." He could not fathom why the North Vietnamese would keep fighting, given the arsenal of weapons the Americans had. He'd heard stories of the North Vietnamese

bringing supplies down on bicycles, moving from one place to another, carrying a few mortars and rounds of ammo on a bamboo pole. "But they did it," he said. "They were committed."

Big Jim finished his tour of duty two months before Oshiro. Before he left, they made a solemn promise to each other. "Once we left Vietnam and went back to the world, we would never see each other again," said Oshiro. "We just didn't want to relate back to what was going on in Vietnam, or some of the things we went through or witnessed."

Oshiro was assigned to work with a new partner. It was nerve-racking without Big Jim. "You get to know a person. You trust the person," Oshiro said. "And then eventually they set you up with another person and then you have to really watch your back for a while, to see how good this person is."

To Oshiro's huge relief, it went well with his new partner. Two months later, he flew back to the United States. "I ended up alive," said Oshiro, "and that's what was important." But he was acutely aware of how many Americans hadn't made it back. "Buddies, and new guys whose names I never got to know," he said, "which haunts one for a lifetime, a lurking shadow." Mixed in with his relief was a terrible sense of guilt. Why had he survived and they hadn't?

Supplies of fresh water and hot food are unloaded from a helicopter at a mountaintop camp thirty miles northwest of Qui Nhon, 1966. Soldiers moved quickly, hoping to get out before snipers could target their helicopter as they left.

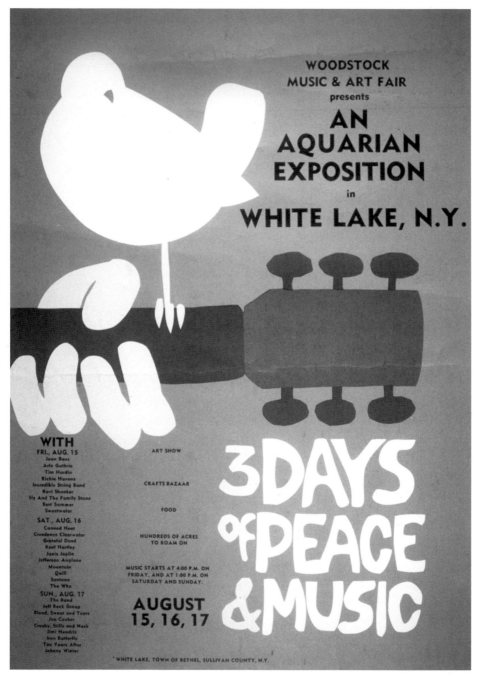

Poster advertising the Woodstock Music and Art Fair, 1969.

AMERICA: PROTEST SINGER

COUNTRY JOE MCDONALD
AUGUST 1969—MARCH 1970

"There is no anti-soldier sentiment in 'Fixin'-to-Die Rag.' Soldiers are doing the job of fighting the war. They are forced to do really dangerous work. It's laborious and tedious, too. The song blames the people who make war happen."

POSTERS WERE PLASTERED on walls and taped on store windows announcing the upcoming Woodstock Music and Art Fair on August 15, 16, and 17. The outdoor concert was joyfully billed as "three days of peace and music." Organizers invited an exhilarating mix of performers: there would be rock and roll, rhythm and blues, folk and country. They were sure it was going to be big, and figured up to 100,000 people would show up.

One band, Country Joe and the Fish, had been invited at the last minute to fill an empty spot on the Sunday program. Country Joe McDonald had jumped at the chance. For the last four years, he had been performing at concerts, antiwar rallies, and marches, but this would be the group's largest audience ever.

Country Joe was a bona fide "red-diaper baby," a kid raised by parents who were card-carrying Communists. To prove his family was patriotic, and because he thought being in uniform would attract girls, Country Joe had joined the navy in 1959 at the age of seventeen. But after a few years, he realized he didn't like the rules and constriction of any rigid organization—not the Communist Party, and not the military. He was glad to get out. In 1965, while he was living in Berkeley, California, he began singing songs at the early protest rallies that had sprung up against the war.

One night at home, he'd picked up his guitar and leaned back in his living-room chair, thinking and dreaming. He strummed some chords, testing them out. Words to a song, "I-Feel-Like-I'm-Fixin'-to-Die Rag," formed into stanzas. In half an hour, he had a whole song pulled together: words, melody, and chords.

Country Joe liked to get to concerts long before he was scheduled to appear so he could see everyone else perform, and Woodstock was no exception. He arrived on Friday, a day ahead of his band, and checked into a motel full of other musicians. Early Saturday morning, he and his manager caught a ride to the concert. The narrow country roads were getting jammed, and they didn't want to get stuck in traffic.

Because he was one of the performers, Country Joe was allowed to hang out on the stage, where people were busy running sound and equipment checks. He and his manager found an out-of-the-way spot on one side of the platform as the roadies and producers got things rolling. Country Joe was shocked by the size of the audience; several hundred thousand people covered the hills as far as he could see, and thousands more were still pouring in.

The music hadn't wrapped up until 2:00 a.m. the night before, while intermittent rain fell. Wet, cold campers had spent the night in soaked sleeping bags, trying to get a little sleep. After slogging through mud in the morning and waiting in long lines for latrines and something to eat, everyone was bleary-eyed and subdued.

The first band started late on Saturday morning, and when they finished, panic set in with the organizers. Where was Santana, the next act? Word spread quickly around the stage: none of the bands was getting through the traffic, now at a dead stop as people abandoned their cars and walked the last few miles to the festival. The organizers asked Country Joe if he'd fill some time doing a solo act.

Members of Jefferson Airplane onstage at Woodstock, 1969. Country Joe McDonald (wearing headband, standing second from right) joins them.

"I don't have a guitar," he said. The huge crowd was intimidating, and besides, he was used to playing electric music with his band.

The organizers were desperate. What was a music festival with no music? Someone found an acoustic guitar and brought it to Country Joe. "I don't have a guitar strap," he said. Someone found a piece of rope, tied it to the guitar, and thrust it at Country Joe.

Song possibilities ran rapid-fire through his mind as he slowly made his way to the middle of the stage and stood behind the mike. He bought a little time as he stood, tuning the unfamiliar guitar. What should he play, solo, with an acoustic guitar? The smells of marijuana, patchouli oil, food, and mud swirled in the air as he tried to calm his nerves.

He was so awed by the size of the crowd, he didn't even notice the "camera pit" at the foot of the stage, or the camera crews perched on high scaffolds, their movie cameras whirring.

Country Joe at Woodstock, 1969.

After strumming a few chords, Country Joe opened with a plaintive lost-love song, "Janis," he'd written after a breakup with singer Janis Joplin. A few people in the audience clapped politely. He played several more songs, but no one seemed to care.

Country Joe walked to the side of the stage and asked his manager if it would be all right to play one of his antiwar songs. Would it be too political, or would that fit in with Woodstock's "peace and love" theme? His manager shrugged. "Nobody's paying any attention to you, so what difference will it make?"

Back in front of the mike, Country Joe launched into "I-Feel-Like-I'm-Fixin'-to-Die Rag."

> Well, c'mon all of you big strong men,
> Uncle Sam needs your help again.
> He's got himself in a terrible jam

Way down yonder in Vietnam.
Put down your books and pick up a gun,
We're gonna have a whole lotta fun.

Very few people in the audience had ever served in the military. Country Joe knew that the rosy scenario young peace protestors had in their minds—that you could just put down your gun and say "peace, man"—was not possible. "I was well aware that you could be put in the brig or shot for treason," he said. His song was loaded with the blunt, sarcastic humor soldiers used to get through their days, following orders that didn't always make sense.

"Listen, people," he said while he strummed. "I don't know how you expect to ever stop the war if you can't sing any better than that . . . I want you to start singin'. Come on!"

Now c'mon mothers throughout the land,
Pack your boys off to Vietnam.
C'mon fathers, don't hesitate.
Send your sons off before it's too late.
Be the first one on your block
To have your boy come home in a box.

His music and attitude worked. As he hit the final chorus, everybody surged to their feet, clapping, whistling, and singing along with him. Now the whole place was *alive*.

And it's one, two, three,
What are we fighting for?
Don't ask me, I don't give a damn,
Next stop is Vietnam;
And it's five, six, seven,
Open up the pearly gates,

Well, there ain't no time to wonder why,
Whoopee! We're all gonna die.

Country Joe raised the guitar high in the air, gave a triumphant wave to the audience, and walked offstage. One of the relieved organizers grabbed him in a tight bear hug.

The three-day concert was supposed to finish Sunday night, but the music kept going all night long as one band after another played. Finally the last performer, Jimi Hendrix, took the stage Monday morning with his band. Hendrix moved smoothly into his set, his white jacket with long blue-beaded tassels swaying with every move

he and his guitar made. His rendition of "The Star-Spangled Banner" brought the audience to a standstill.

The last chord from Hendrix's guitar echoed off the hills, and the concert was over. People headed out, and the exhausted organizers stared in disbelief at the trash left behind. The filmmakers packed up their cameras and rushed to the editing room to see what kind of footage they had.

When the film *Woodstock* came out the following March, it screened to sold-out audiences everywhere. Overnight, "Fixin'-to-Die," with its sarcastic, memorable lyrics, became an anthem of the antiwar movement, sung at protests and marches across the United States.

Joe Cocker's band setting up for their afternoon performance in front of an immense crowd, August 17, 1969. A downpour from a huge thunderstorm forced a break in the concert, after which Country Joe and the Fish appeared.

Lily Lee Adams after graduating from nursing school, 1968.

VIETNAM: NURSE

LILY LEE ADAMS
IN COUNTRY OCTOBER 1969—OCTOBER 1970

"When I witnessed the carnage, the suffering, I blamed God and was so angry at him for letting war happen. To let grandmas, children, babies, soldiers, mothers, and fathers suffer so. I said, 'God, you're dead.' But every time I had a patient, I'd be praying to God to keep him alive, because I didn't want them to die on me."

ON HER FIRST day in triage at an army hospital in Vietnam, Lily Lee Adams was told to stay out of the way, watch, and learn. Around her, doctors, nurses, and medics sprang into gear, hanging IV bottles on poles and throwing extra tourniquets around their shoulders.

The door flew open, and two men rushed in with a stretcher between them, set it down on two waiting sawhorses, then hurried back out. Someone cut off the patient's muddy, bloody uniform, and Adams saw his legs had been blown off at the thighs. A doctor started an IV, while a nurse tried to question the infantryman for his name, rank, and serial number. Adams was horrified. "I froze," she said. "The guy had been blown up, basically."

More helicopters landed, bringing another batch of patients, and then another. "Coming in, they just kept coming in," said Adams. Nothing in her experience—her difficult childhood, her previous work with injured patients—had prepared her for this kind of hell on earth.

Shortly after Adams was born, her mother had died. Her father ran a laundry business and couldn't take care of her, and she'd been sent to live with a foster family until she was eight years old. When her father remarried, she'd gone to live with him and her stepmother, who was harsh and punishing. The most peaceful place for her, where she felt safe and protected, was the Catholic Church. She thought she'd be a nun when she grew up, and live a quiet, contemplative life serving God. But in high school, she got interested in boys and realized she wouldn't make a good nun.

Nursing and caring for others appealed to her. In 1965, right after high school, she enrolled in nursing school in New York. School was rigorous, but Adams didn't mind. She had a plan: when she got out of nursing school, she'd move to San Francisco and get a job in a hospital. There were many Chinese there, like her father, and Italians like her mother's family. There would be people in San Francisco who looked and thought as she did. Her favorite song, "San Francisco (Be Sure to Wear Some Flowers in Your Hair)," became a musical promise: there would be gentle people in San Francisco, people against the war, who gathered for love-ins and peaceful protests.

During Adams's second year in nursing school in New York, a recruiter from the army came around, soliciting student nurses to join. Adams was skeptical. She wore delicate "love beads" around her neck and was in wholehearted agreement with the protestors who wanted America out of Vietnam. The recruiter assured her that army nurses volunteered to serve in Vietnam; they weren't ordered to go. Adams signed up.

After becoming a registered nurse, Adams was assigned to work at Fort Ord, in California. She liked the hospital and the routines, but in August 1969, she was sent back home to recover after a bad bout of pancreatitis left her weak and exhausted. Some of her friends who dropped by to visit had just been to the Woodstock music festival a few weeks earlier. They talked about the weekend as if they'd had a religious experience, and Adams felt she'd missed something life-changing. Before they left, they gave her a copy of *Life* magazine full of wonderful stories and pictures of the weekend. She spent hours staring at the photographs and imagining she had been there.

Shortly after returning to Fort Ord, Adams received orders to deploy to Vietnam. She was shocked: the recruiter had lied to her. She immediately went to talk to the chief nurse, who told Adams they were desperate for good nurses in Vietnam. Adams felt betrayed by the recruiter, but she decided not to fight the orders.

In late October 1969, Adams flew to Vietnam and waited at an army base for her assignment. She was miserable. What had she gotten herself into? The one place she could get a respite from the heat was the air-conditioned officers' club. She'd get a Coke and take it to a table, sipping it slowly. Most of the nurses didn't like to hang

Adams (front row, second from left) with her medical team, 1969. She sits next to the team's Vietnamese interpreter (in flowered dress).

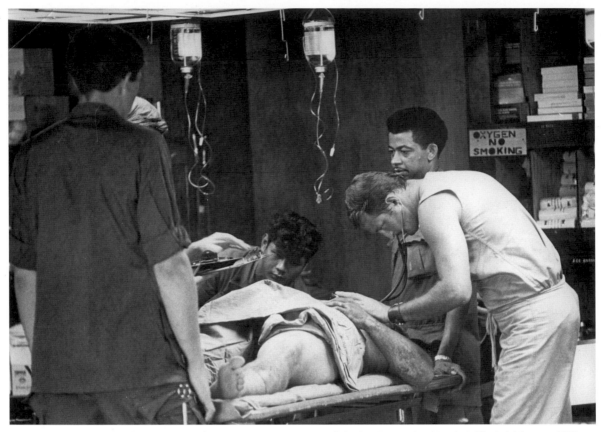

A doctor checks the heartbeat of a casualty in the emergency room of the 91st Evacuation Hospital, Chu Lai, Vietnam, 1970.

out in the officers' club with the drinking, flirtatious men. "These idiots came up and made fools of themselves," said Adams, when she just wanted to be left alone. But one officer, Captain Jerry Denny, quietly befriended her. He'd come in at the same time she had and already missed his wife and two young sons terribly. He didn't see how he was going to stand being away from them for a year.

Adams and Denny talked for hours in the officers' club. He told her the insignia on his uniform meant he was a crewmember on a helicopter that sprayed Agent Orange. "Well, if it kills trees in twenty-four hours," she asked him, "aren't you afraid it will kill you?" He wasn't worried about Agent Orange, but going up in a helicopter every day in a war zone was dangerous, and they both knew it. Adams promised if he didn't make it back, she'd find his wife and sons and tell them how much he loved them.

Adams and two of the other nurses were assigned to the 12th Evacuation Hospital at Cu Chi and shipped out on the same cargo plane as Denny. Adams was over-whelmed when they arrived at the 25th Infantry Division at Cu Chi, about twenty miles northwest of Saigon. The compound was enormous. It was like a small city, laid out on a grid with mess halls, stores, bars, movie theaters, and even swimming pools. Trucks roared up and down the streets, and planes and helicopters constantly landed and took off right overhead.

No one was there to meet them. Denny refused to leave until the chief nurse arrived and said she'd personally show them to the nurses' quarters. It was hard for Adams to say good-bye to Denny. "Here we are, in a war zone," she said, "and he is still a gentleman. He was making sure that me and my companions were doing okay."

The head nurse took them over to the nurses' barracks. Adams had her own tiny room, just barely big enough for a single bed and a bureau. But with the schedule of twelve-hour workdays six days a week, she was assured she wouldn't do anything more than eat and sleep during her time off.

After putting away her clothes, Adams decided to take a walk around the compound to orient herself. An officer came out of a building and yelled at her, "Sandy, come in here." Adams looked at him, startled, and asked, "Who is Sandy?"

"I'm sorry, I'm sorry," he replied in embarrassment. "I thought you were Sandy, our Vietnamese interpreter." *Oh God*, she thought, *be prepared for the rest of the year to be mistaken for something you're not.*

After her first few days of orientation in triage, Adams was moved into the intensive care unit (ICU). Half of the patients were amputations—they'd had one or more arms or legs blown off. The straightforward amputations were flown right to Japan for treatment in the modern hospital, but the more severely wounded had to be stabilized for the trip over.

The other half of the ward were burn patients, people injured by explosions or fires. Adams and the other nurses had to remove their dressings and put fresh antibiotic ointment over the burned area every twenty-four hours.

Many shifts she was kept running from one patient to another, making sure amputees were stable, caring for the burn patients. The soldiers were mostly eighteen or nineteen years old. She did her best to give them a little respite from the war zone: she wore her love beads, put ribbons in her hair, and dabbed perfume behind her ears every morning.

But it was the quiet, slow times that tore at her emotionally. Her patients wanted to tell her about feeling their lives were ruined now that their bodies were, their phantom limb pain, their fear of suffering and dying. She heard about the family dogs they missed, parents who were ill, fiancées they figured would no longer want them. Her love beads and perfume seemed so irrelevant.

A soldier dropped by one day wearing a patch she recognized from Captain Denny's uniform. She eagerly asked how Denny was doing. Sadness washed over his face. "He got shot down," the man replied. Adams couldn't believe it. She remembered how kind he was to her when she'd first arrived, overwhelmed and miserable. And now he would never get home to the wife and sons he missed. It made her angry at God, fed up with everything about the war. How could he let this all happen?

But week after week, as she worked on casualties, she prayed. *Not this one, not this other one either. Please help me save these lives. They are so young.* She'd pray, *Don't let them die on my watch.* Some were just too badly wounded to survive. It was a bittersweet moment for Adams. "When they did die, I experienced a peace I never knew. I could tell the moment they left me, like a puff of energy was turned loose," she said. "When a soldier died, I felt as if he were looking out for me as well. So I was stuck between blaming God and asking for his help, his grace."

One day two Vietnamese brothers around seven or eight years old were brought in with severe phosphorus burns. Adams hated phosphorus, which was only meant to be used to mark targets for artillery. The phosphorus would keep burning and burning, right through muscle and bone. "You could smell the flesh, because it didn't stop burning," said Adams. "We had to put stuff on it to neutralize it. But you could still smell it in the air." She tried her best to save them, but both boys died. "They had no chance," said Adams. "That was phosphorus." She felt terribly guilty at her relief they had died, and were no longer suffering.

The ICU with the lingering burns and grievously wounded patients got to be too difficult, and she asked to be transferred back to the ER to do triage. Patients would come in and get moved on quickly. It was a much better place for her, where she felt useful. Decisions were made on technical grounds—who could be saved?—and not emotional ones.

"Besides casualties," said Adams, "we also got motorcycle accidents, women in labor, all kinds of stuff which happened to the locals." It didn't even bother her that when they treated Vietnamese, they called them "gooks" and "slopes."

One of the engineers on the base kept bringing Vietnamese children into triage who needed treatment. One day he brought in a baby with an abscess. The doctor refused to take care of the baby. "I totally lost it," said Adams. "I started yelling at him. 'You are going to refuse to take care of a baby? What is this baby going to do to you? If you don't want to take care of the baby, I know doctors that would love to.'" The doctor was shocked at her anger. "Wait a minute," he said. "Wait, wait! I changed my mind."

After the doctor took care of the abscess, Adams asked the engineer, "Where are you getting these babies from?"

"Rose Orphanage," he replied. "It's a Catholic orphanage. You want to go see it?"

Adams jumped at the chance. "Yes," she said. "Anything to get me out of here.

Orphaned children, some with American fathers and Vietnamese mothers, eat a meal in an orphanage, 1972. The mixed heritage American and Vietnamese children were known as mỹ lai.

Anything to get my brain going somewhere else other than casualties."

At the orphanage, she'd play with the kids and point out any who needed medicine or medical care. Being half Asian was helpful. "I wasn't a stranger," she said. "The kids were more friendly toward me because I was Asian-looking." Being with the nuns was comforting, even though they couldn't speak the same language. "The nuns were so loving and so sweet," she said. "So caring." When she wrote home, she asked to be sent used children's clothes, which she took to the orphanage. The engineers helped too, bringing needed supplies and food with them. Adams was surprised to hear that the North Vietnamese were bringing rice to the orphanage. "They would steal from the Vietnamese that they killed, or whatever," she said. "And they would bring the rice over to the orphanage for the children."

No one wanted to see children go hungry, no matter what their politics.

One day a North Vietnamese soldier was brought into triage, and Adams was asked to take care of him. At first, she didn't want to. He wasn't an innocent civilian. "He was the enemy," she said, "and he probably killed a bunch of my people." But she didn't refuse. As she began caring for him, her feelings gradually shifted. "I started to work hard to keep him alive," she said. "Because he was a human being, number one. And number two, they were saying if we can keep this guy alive, we can get answers from him, because he has a buddy on the other side of the hospital. And their stories have to be the same."

Five or six hours later, the interrogator and an interpreter arrived. Adams moved swiftly to stand in between the interrogator and her patient. She'd seen some of these prisoners after the interrogators got through with them.

"I've been working my ass off to keep this man alive," she said. "What are you going to do to him?" The interrogator assured her he wasn't going to do anything to the prisoner. "You ask them questions," he said, "and they are in no shape to tell you anything else. They know that we've captured their buddies. They know they have to tell the truth."

Adams listened intently to the patient's answers: where he was from, how long he had served, what he knew about NVA plans. When the interrogation was over, she asked the interpreter, "Would you mind asking him a question for me? He doesn't have to answer it; it won't change my care for him. I want to know how he feels about

the war." With her affinity for the Americans holding protests at home, she hoped the soldier would say something to help her understand why Americans had to fight so hard against the Communists.

"He looked me straight in the eye and said, 'If I could march in Hanoi like you are marching in Washington, DC, I would be doing it.'" Adams was shocked that an enemy soldier was so strongly against the war he wished he could march in the streets of North Vietnam's capital city. She had thought all the NVA soldiers were dedicated to the Communist cause. She asked

A Viet Cong suspect, whose injured leg was bandaged by a US Marines medic, is carried to an interrogation area in a battle zone, 1965.

how old he was: nineteen. *Just like my patients and feeling the same way*, thought Adams. *That doesn't help me. It just makes my antiwar feelings stronger.*

One day a patient with his arm in a cast walked into the room where she was working and asked her to come outside for a minute. Curious, Adams followed him. Standing around outside were ten men in faded, worn uniforms. It turned out they were soldiers who worked with military scout dogs and lived on the far side of the base. They invited her to come visit on her next day off.

Adams took them up on their offer. It felt good to change out of her uniform into regular clothes and walk across the compound to where they lived with their dogs.

There were about twenty dog handlers all together. Each soldier was paired up with a dog to track enemies through the jungle, search villages, and walk point looking for booby traps or snipers. Half of the soldiers were black, mostly from Chicago, the other half white, mostly from California. The guys from Chicago listened to R&B, while the Californians were into acid rock. Both groups would blast their music as loud as they could—the Temptations and Marvin Gaye trying to drown out Jefferson Airplane and Janis Joplin. But everyone listened to Jimi Hendrix.

Adams couldn't believe it when she stepped into one of the handlers' huts. There were hippie posters all over the walls. The guys loved to talk about music and the good things that were happening back home. Living by the perimeter, they got by without the strict military scrutiny she was used to. She could forget, for the moment, she was in the middle of a war.

"There was a whole bunch of them I made friends with," said Adams. "We were all hippies." After a long shift, she'd head over with a reel-to-reel tape of the Woodstock concert to share. Joints would pass hand to hand as they all listened to the music. The songs gave her a rare feeling of peace.

Finally, Adams's long year in Vietnam was over, and she was sent back to the Oakland Army Base in California. The next day she was processed out of the army.

Still in her uniform, Adams took a bus across the bay to San Francisco, where a friend was going to pick her up. But people kept shooting dirty looks at her as she waited on the street. "Everybody—I swear, everybody—was giving me these awful looks," she said. "I'm looking at my uniform. Is it right? Are things crooked?"

She went back inside the bus depot and called her friend. "Get out of your uniform," he said, "and get into civilian clothes. They are beating up people who are in military uniform." He explained to her how much more angry people were about the war than a year ago when she went over.

"But *I'm* not the war," Adams replied. "I went to war because I was sent there. I saved lives. I didn't kill babies." She couldn't believe it. This was San Francisco, the home of peace and love, and wearing flowers in your hair. But she hurried into the restroom to change anyway.

"Everybody ignored me when I walked out," she said.

Private First Class Ronald T. Roane and his dog Hobo look for booby traps, snipers, and other dangers, 1969. Around 5,000 dogs were trained in the US and served in Vietnam during the war.

Vietnam veterans, some wearing their combat uniforms, protest outside the US Capitol, smashing toy guns, 1971. About a thousand veterans took part in the weeklong antiwar demonstration in Washington, DC.

AMERICA:
PRESIDENT AND COMMANDER IN CHIEF

RICHARD M. NIXON
OCTOBER 1969—AUGUST 1974

"If, when the chips are down, the world's most powerful nation, the United States of America, acts like a pitiful, helpless giant, the forces of totalitarianism and anarchy will threaten free nations and free institutions throughout the world."

ON OCTOBER 15, 1969, cities across the United States erupted in protest. The Moratorium to End the War in Vietnam had been planned for months. It was one of the largest and best-organized demonstrations yet, bringing out tens of thousands of new protestors. Nixon was determined to hide how much the successful Moratorium bothered him. To steady his nerves, he scribbled an anxious reminder to himself on a speech he was preparing: "Don't get rattled—don't waver—don't react."

A few weeks later, Nixon sat at his desk in front of television cameras reading his speech and calling on the "great silent majority" of his fellow Americans to support him. He vowed to keep his military commitment to Vietnam, and took sharp aim at the protestors. "The more divided we are at home, the less likely the enemy is to negotiate at Paris," he said. "Because let us understand: North Vietnam cannot defeat or humiliate the United States. Only Americans can do that." Nixon didn't admit that he was carrying on his massive, clandestine bombing of Cambodia. Or that, even as the Paris Peace Accords continued, he had sent Henry Kissinger to conduct separate talks with the North Vietnamese without informing the South Vietnamese.

But demonstrators, determined to keep up the pressure on Nixon, held a second Moratorium march on November 15. Over half a million people attended in Washington, DC, alone. Nixon claimed to be unconcerned by the protest and spent the day at the White House meeting with four of his top advisors.

Protestors were fairly quiet during the winter, and Nixon decided to act before they started up again. On April 20, 1970, he announced he would withdraw another 150,000 troops from Vietnam. He figured the news would "drop a bombshell on the gathering spring storm of antiwar protest." But just ten days later, with intelligence reports showing an increase in North Vietnamese activity in Cambodia, Nixon made a stunning announcement. He had decided he would "go for broke" and send American ground troops along with ARVN troops to attack NVA sanctuaries in Cambodia. Once again, he soberly addressed Americans in a televised speech. "It is not our power but our will and character that is being tested tonight," he said. "If we fail to meet this challenge, all other nations will be on notice that despite its overwhelming power the United States, when a real crisis comes, will be found wanting." He assured his audience that as soon as the enemy sanctuaries had been eliminated and NVA military supplies destroyed, American troops would be withdrawn.

Although Nixon insisted that this was not an invasion of Cambodia but just a military operation, the announcement galvanized the antiwar movement. Across the United States, it caused fresh demonstrations, infuriating Nixon. He could no longer control his disdain for those who opposed his policies and he lashed out. The protestors were, he said dismissively, "bums."

His "bums" comment made newspaper headlines across the country and brought angry crowds onto streets and campuses in protest. At Kent State University in Ohio, tensions escalated so much that the governor sent in the National Guard. Over the next few days, protestors threw rocks and bottles, broke windows, and set fire to a military building on campus. On Monday, May 4, 1970, the students were ordered to disperse. Many refused to comply. National Guardsmen with fixed bayonets and guns

The Ohio National Guard moves in on students during a Vietnam War protest at Kent State University, 1970.

on "lock and load" opened fire. In thirteen seconds they fired sixty-seven rounds, injuring nine and killing four. It had come to this: American military were shooting down unarmed Americans.

The deaths stunned Nixon. He couldn't get the newspaper images of the dead out of his mind. As a coast-to-coast call went out for even more demonstrations, he worried: *Would this tragedy become the cause of scores of others?*

Nixon wrote personal letters to the parents of the four dead protestors. It was a well-meant, hopeless gesture. The anguished father of one of the dead girls bitterly told a reporter, "My child was not a bum."

Hundreds of American universities, colleges, and high schools shut down for the week as students staged impassioned protests. On Saturday, May 9, 100,000 demonstrators spontaneously took to the streets of Washington, DC. Police, fearing the protests would turn violent, parked a protective barricade of buses head-to-tail around the White House.

Army troops from the 82nd Airborne were trucked into the city and hidden in the basement of the Executive Office Building, right next door to the White House. If the protest became more than the police could handle, the fully armed troops could be brought onto the streets instantly. One administration official went down to the basement and was alarmed by the men and their military equipment. "They're lying on the floor," he said, "leaning on their packs and their helmets and their cartridge belts and their rifles cocked, and you're thinking, 'This can't be the United States of America. This is not the greatest free democracy in the world. This is a nation at war with itself.'"

Despite the deep divisions in the country, Nixon moved forward with military operations in Cambodia. The ground troops, reinforced by heavy air support, destroyed the North Vietnamese sanctuaries, and confiscated weapons, rice, and medical equipment. By the end of June, Nixon pulled the American troops out of Cambodia, but continued his secretive policies of bombing Cambodia and having Kissinger meet with the North Vietnamese. Meanwhile, the Paris Peace Accords went nowhere, and public opinion kept turning further against the war.

ON SUNDAY MORNING, June 13, 1971, Nixon was in an especially good mood. The day before, his daughter, Tricia, had been married in the Rose Garden at the White House. Despite the threat of rain, the ceremony had gone off perfectly. But within hours on Sunday morning Nixon's worried aides were calling him. On the front page of *The New York Times*, two columns over from a photo of him walking Tricia to the altar, was an article with the headline "Vietnam Archive: Pentagon Study Traces 3 Decades of Growing U. S. Involvement." A former Pentagon employee named Daniel Ellsberg had illegally leaked highly classified information to the *Times*. At first, Nixon wasn't very concerned. After all, the study only went up through 1968, to the end of Johnson's presidency. There was nothing in it to incriminate him.

But as he thought about it, Nixon got angry. Who would release government secrets like this? He couldn't believe a trusted Pentagon employee with top security clearance had leaked information to the press. "This is a treasonable action on the part of the bastards that put it out," he ranted to Kissinger later that afternoon on the phone. "And people have got to be put to the torch for this sort of thing. This is terrible."

On Monday, there was a second article, then a third the following day. The secret study, quickly dubbed the Pentagon Papers, shocked Americans. Ellsberg, who had once supported the war, now hoped releasing the information would force an end to

A Vietnam veteran who opposes the war throws his medal over a fence that kept protesters away from the Capitol, 1971. Some veterans were angry that their sacrifices in Vietnam had been for nothing; others were heartbroken over the death tolls. The demonstrators' defiance made a strong statement: We reject this war.

it. He knew he faced years—maybe the rest of his life—in prison. He was willing to accept the consequences of his illegal action.

Nixon tried to block further publication of the Pentagon Papers through the courts, but he lost. And just like President Johnson before him, Nixon hated to lose. Though Ellsberg had turned himself in and faced criminal charges, that wasn't enough for Nixon. He was determined to trash Ellsberg's reputation.

Nixon authorized the creation of a Special Investigations Unit. It was a fancy, official-sounding name for a small, sneaky group. They called themselves the "Plumbers," since they were going to fix "leaks" in the White House. The men got to work examining Ellsberg's life, looking for anything that would humiliate or discredit him.

On the night of September 3, the Plumbers ransacked Ellsberg's psychiatrist's office, hoping to find something embarrassing in the files on Ellsberg. But the break-in was a bust: they found no record of Ellsberg's visits.

It would have been a good idea to call off the Plumbers before they got caught, but no one did.

They lay quiet for a while, then their focus shifted to helping Nixon get reelected to a second term. In June 1972, they broke into the Democratic National Committee headquarters at the Watergate complex in Washington, DC. A few weeks earlier they had installed listening devices on two phones, and one device wasn't working. They went back to repair it and were caught red-handed.

Nixon ordered the break-in covered up. It worked. At least, long enough for Nixon to get reelected on November 7, 1972.

A month later, Kissinger returned from more secret negotiations with the North Vietnamese and reported to Nixon that his latest attempts had broken down once again. Kissinger, frustrated by his inability to wring concessions from the Communists, told Nixon they were "tawdry, miserable, filthy people. . . . They never, never do anything that isn't tawdry." He encouraged Nixon to "start bombing the bejesus out of them."

Nixon did. He ordered a brutal bombardment of North Vietnam, soon known as the Christmas bombing. Over the next eleven days, the US Air Force flew 729

From the Oval Office, Nixon announces US military forces have left Vietnam as agreed in the Paris Peace Accords, March 29, 1973.

nighttime bombing raids over Hanoi and the harbor of Haiphong. These were the largest heavy bomber strikes since World War II, and forced North Vietnam to make concessions at the negotiating table. On January 27, 1973, delegates from the United States, North Vietnam, South Vietnam, and the Viet Cong formally signed the Paris Peace Accords. The North Vietnamese agreed to accept South Vietnam as a separate country, and a cease-fire was established.

On the same day, in Washington, DC, the Selective Service announced the end of the draft. From now on, the American military would be an all-volunteer force.

By the end of March, the last US combat troops pulled out of Vietnam, leaving ten thousand Americans: military advisors, Marines to protect US installations, and non-military personnel. Nixon solemnly promised to defend South Vietnam with air strikes if North Vietnam violated the terms of the Paris Peace Accords.

Within a year, the Communists did attack, breaking the treaty. But Nixon was powerless to help South Vietnam. Congress had prohibited him from any more bombing in Cambodia and limited his right to wage war. The truth was also coming out about Nixon's cover-up of the Watergate break-in. The complicated chain of events, known as the Watergate scandal, included hush money and destroyed evidence. The cover-up was a serious crime: obstruction of justice. To avoid impeachment by the House of Representatives, Nixon resigned on August 9, 1974, the first American president ever to do so. Vice President Gerald R. Ford was immediately sworn in as the new president.

President Gerald R. Ford (right) *and Vice President Nelson Rockefeller listen to advice on the evacuation of Saigon, 1975.*

AMERICA:
PRESIDENT AND COMMANDER IN CHIEF

GERALD R. FORD
MARCH 1975—APRIL 1975

"We couldn't just cut and run. We had to consider the people of Vietnam and what might happen to them, especially those who had supported us."

THE NEW PRESIDENT faced a daunting task in Vietnam. It was clear the North Vietnamese would continue their relentless efforts to unify the country under Communist rule, and the situation was deteriorating rapidly. In March 1975, the NVA launched a final offensive, pouring down into South Vietnam. The city of Hue fell, then Da Nang. Refugees flooded the roads, desperately looking for safety as Communist troops pushed south toward Saigon in their final "Ho Chi Minh Campaign."

In late March, Ford sent the Army chief of staff, General Frederick Weyand, to Vietnam. The president wanted an honest, firsthand report on how serious conditions actually were in South Vietnam. Ford warned Weyand not to convey a message of American weakness. "You are not going over there to lose," he told the general, "but to be tough and see what we can do."

Weyand returned on April 5 and quickly debriefed Ford on his trip. Weyand admitted the situation in Vietnam looked dire, but held out a thin thread of possibility:

maybe the South Vietnamese government could be propped up with more financial help.

Ford made a last-ditch appeal to Congress for economic aid to South Vietnam, but his request was refused. Congress, like the American public, wanted nothing more to do with the war. There would be no attempt at a reprieve for South Vietnam from America. It was time to get out.

By mid-April, the collapse of the South Vietnamese government was imminent. In addition to several thousand Americans still in Vietnam, there were at least a hundred thousand "at risk" Vietnamese who had worked closely with the Americans. Many of them would be imprisoned or killed if the Communists took over. Ford worried about how many he could get out of the country.

Over the next few weeks, Air Force planes made flight after flight, carrying Americans and "at risk" South Vietnamese out of the country. Navy ships massed offshore, and desperate Vietnamese headed for them in small boats. Saigon, under sporadic artillery shelling and surrounded by the Communists, was in complete chaos.

President Ford meets with Secretary of State Henry Kissinger (right) *and Army Chief of Staff General Frederick Weyand, 1975.*

Overloaded trucks and buses stall in a traffic jam as thousands of civilians and military personnel flee from Hue to Da Nang as North Vietnamese and Viet Cong forces advance, 1975.

VIETNAM: REFUGEE

HOA THI NGUYEN
MARCH 1975–APRIL 1975

"We're not going to run anymore. If we run over there we're going to die anyway, and my uncle is not going to be able to find our bodies."

FROM INSIDE THE HOUSE, eighteen-year-old Hoa thi Nguyen could hear panicked people on the street running and shouting. Huddled with her parents and six younger sisters and brothers, Nguyen peered out the window. The radio in the living room crackled with bad news. The nearby city of Hue had fallen to the Communists the day before, March 26. Now the NVA was heading straight for Da Nang, intent on taking over the city. Frantic refugees from the northern provinces filled Da Nang's streets.

As the Communists advanced, they had overrun one ARVN fighting unit after another. Routed from their positions in total disarray, tens of thousands of South Vietnamese soldiers deserted. They'd kept their weapons, but stripped off their tell-tale uniforms, begged or stolen clothes, and joined the tide of refugees fleeing toward Saigon. Some desperate civilians and soldiers were looting stores, stealing food from shopkeepers, callously killing to get what they needed.

No one in Nguyen's family was safe from the Communists. Her father had been in the South Vietnamese military and worked with the Americans at the Da Nang Air Force base. Sometimes Americans had even come to the house. *They will cut my dad's*

Thirteen-year-old Hoa thi Nguyen (far left) stands with her parents and siblings. Nguyen, her sister Yen (second from right), and their mother escaped. The others were left behind in Da Nang. Trai and Lai, who also escaped, had not been born when this photo was taken, 1970.

neck, or hang him, she thought. Quickly, she took the photos of her father with the Americans off the walls and destroyed them. The radio announcer's voice was shrill: the Communists would show no mercy. Neighbors rushed over, repeating more rumors: all the children would be slaughtered.

Nguyen knew the Communists might force her to carry a gun and fight for them. Even worse things could happen to a young woman at the hands of the victorious Communist troops. She couldn't stand to think about it. Her family had to escape, as soon as they could. With the American troops no longer fighting, what could her father do to protect her and her sisters and brothers? What could she do?

Ever since the third grade, when her father made her quit school and help at home, Nguyen had been taking care of her siblings. Every morning Nguyen went to the city well to fill heavy buckets of water and bring them home to keep their cistern filled. She helped her mother cook and clean. At the nearby open-air market, she bargained for fish, chicken, rice, vegetables, and salt. As a teenager, Nguyen found odd jobs to do for the Americans on the nearby base, digging ditches and fixing potholes in roads. It didn't matter how hard the work was, she would do it.

Only a few days after Hue fell, the Communists had completely surrounded Da Nang, cutting off the main road south to Saigon. Rocket fire came in from the perimeter. Desperate to get out, thousands of refugees headed to the airport and massed on the runway, making it impossible for planes to take off. The only way out was by boat. On the radio, announcers repeated the news that big American ships were waiting offshore and more were coming. They would pick up South Vietnamese soldiers and civilians, and take them down to Saigon, to safety.

People swarmed the docks and beaches. If they were lucky, they could crowd onto an American boat or barge, or pay gold to get a fisherman to take them out to where the big ships waited. Roving bands of Viet Cong appeared on the streets, shooting the traitorous Vietnamese heading for the waiting American ships.

Nguyen's father told her to kill, pluck, and cook one of their chickens, so everyone could have rice and a little meat. They waited until dark, then hurried down to the beach and tried to get a boat out to the big American ships. The hours passed slowly as they crouched and lay on the sandy dirt, waiting. The baby of the family, Lai, was only two months old, and Nguyen and her mother were careful to keep her quiet so they didn't attract any attention. There were more desperate armed men here, roaming the beach and robbing anyone carrying money or gold, even food, as they tried to escape.

At dawn, discouraged and afraid after being unable to find a boat ride, they slipped back home. They tried again the next two nights, but had no luck as the NVA and the Viet Cong tightened their grip on the city. Artillery hammered the neighborhoods, and sporadic firefights broke out.

The fourth night, a different chance to get out appeared. Nguyen's uncle, Linh Huynh, lived nearby with his wife and four children. Huynh had an escape plan that might work for them all. He was in the ARVN Special Forces and worked as a driver for a Vietnamese commander, a man they called the "big guy." Tonight the commander would be evacuating the Special Forces and their families. Huynh promised to see if he could get Nguyen's family out with his.

After the sun went down, Nguyen's family headed for Huynh's house. Huynh left, and they waited and waited. Shooting broke out in the neighborhood, and artillery exploded nearby. There was no chance Huynh could make it back. Finally the fighting stopped, but still Huynh didn't appear. There weren't enough beds for everyone, so Nguyen's father and the three oldest of her siblings headed home in the dark. They would come back in the morning. Nguyen, her mother, her eleven-year-old sister, Yen, her three-year-old brother Trai, and baby Lai settled down to sleep.

At two in the morning, Huynh crept quietly into the house. He'd managed to drive back in an old American military jeep that the "big guy" let him take. Huynh's family and Nguyen, her mother, and three siblings sneaked silently out of the house and packed into the jeep. Huynh didn't dare turn on the headlights. He drove as fast as he could, peering ahead into the pitch-black darkness. They hurtled past huge trucks full of NVA soldiers, coming so close that one scraped Yen's arm where it stuck out beneath the canvas siding. She screamed in pain but was immediately hushed.

Finally they made it to the chaotic, crowded waterfront, where Huynh's commander was loading people onto a barge tied at the pier. As Huynh's and Nguyen's families were swept forward onto the pier in the packed, unruly crowd, Nguyen balked. What about her father and the rest of her family? She didn't want to leave without them.

The commander could barely control the shoving crowd, which was desperate to get aboard. Nguyen saw him grab a woman by the hair and throw her to the ground, then fire his pistol in the air. "The big guy said if anybody doesn't do what he says and get on the boat," Nguyen said, "he'll shoot them right there." She had no choice but to get on without the rest of her family.

The barge didn't take them to the ship, but headed south instead. Nguyen didn't know why, only that they were headed away from the NVA and toward safety. The motor made a low, steady hum, but the refugees barely spoke. There was no water, no food, no place to lie down, just enough room to squat or sit. The sun rose and beat down on them, and still they traveled. Eighteen hours after leaving the port, the barge turned in to Cam Ranh Bay. Everyone disembarked to drink and eat. They stretched out that night wherever they could: on the beach, under tarps, and in old shipping containers. Early in the morning, they were crammed back on the barge for another long day in the sun, heading south to safety. Finally they made it all the way to the port at Saigon, more than five hundred nautical miles south of Da Nang.

They went to stay with a friend of Huynh's, but when they got there, the house was already overcrowded. Only Huynh and his family could remain. Huynh took Nguyen and her family to the Long Thanh refugee camp by bus and left them there, promising he would be in touch. The first night they lay on the open ground with no shelter. The Red Cross brought plastic tarps and blankets from its headquarters in Saigon, as well as a little water, rice, and meat, but not nearly enough.

Nguyen's mother was overwhelmed. Her husband and three of her children were hundreds of miles away in Da Nang, with the entire North Vietnamese Army between them. She sat unmoving for hours at a time. She didn't respond, even to baby Lai's weak cries of

Using a gangplank hastily hammered together from wooden boards, refugees from Da Nang disembark from the US Military Sealift Command ship Pioneer Contender *at Cam Ranh Bay, 1975.*

hunger. Nguyen had to put Lai in her mother's arms and make her nurse the baby. Nguyen said to herself, *I have to be a man now, and take care of my family.* It was all on her shoulders.

Wealthy people in Saigon, hearing about the desperate plight of the refugees, drove out to the camp or came by bus, bringing water and food. Refugees mobbed any new arrival, hoping to get something. Whenever Nguyen saw a crowd, she would push and shove to the middle and stick out her hand to grab at any food being held out. She was determined to keep her family from starving.

Like other children in the camp, her siblings were dehydrated, hungry, and exhausted. After ten days in the camp, both Trai and Lai came down with chicken pox. Lai was hit the hardest. She was covered in sores, and pus glued her eyelids shut. There was no water to clean her face, so Nguyen and Yen walked out into the jungle where the ground was wet, and dug a hole with a broken piece of pottery. They waited while it slowly filled up with muddy water. Nguyen carried the water back in a plastic pail and let the mud settle out so she could boil it and wash her sister's eyelids.

Just days later, a battle erupted between the NVA and ARVN close to the camp. Nguyen threw their food in a bag and grabbed Trai. Her mother took baby Lai. Yen had to stick close and make sure she was always with them. They ran with the crowd of refugees, heading toward the safety of Saigon. Nguyen kept an anxious watch on Yen, afraid she would get knocked over and trampled, or lost in the crowd. The sound of machine-gun fire and artillery shells falling nearby pushed them forward. No one could stop to help anyone who fell.

Suddenly Nguyen realized her mother was not with her. She spun around, holding tight to Trai. With Yen right behind her, Nguyen ran back against the oncoming crush of refugees. She found her mother and Lai on the ground, people stumbling over and around them. Nguyen grabbed Lai and pulled her mother to her feet. To Nguyen's astonishment, they weren't badly hurt.

Nguyen kept her family going as night settled over the jungle, and the nearby shelling continued. Gradually they fell behind the other refugees. Nguyen dropped the bag of food she was carrying. She didn't care about what they would eat later. She could only think about getting her family through each minute, each hour of this nightmare.

In the darkness, a barricade loomed before them, blocking the road that led to a bridge across a river. Nguyen had to choose which way to go. She made a split-second decision, and led her family into the rice paddy on one side. She didn't realize the rest of the fleeing refugees had gone the other way.

They hadn't gotten far when a flash of illumination from a flare revealed dozens of NVA soldiers on the far side of the rice paddy. They were running and shooting at South Vietnamese troops on the other side of the road. Her family had run right between the two armies. *Oh my God*, thought Nguyen, *we are going to die*. She told her mother it was no use to run any farther, then she fainted.

It was morning when Nguyen came to. She lay still. There wasn't a sound, not even a single bird. Then she heard the growl of a truck engine coming down the road, and sat up. Her mother was on one side of her, her sisters and brother on the other. Everyone was still alive. The truck heading toward them was full of ARVN troops. Dead bodies were sprawled on the ground near them in the rice paddy. The battle was over, but Nguyen was afraid there might be NVA soldiers left behind, ready to take aim at anyone that moved, or that a nervous South Vietnamese soldier might shoot them. Those were the chances they'd have to take. They had to get to Saigon, where the ARVN was in control.

No one fired at them as they walked single file along a path through the rice paddy. They were just women and children, on the run.

After several hours of walking, they came to a bigger road where they could catch a bus the rest of the way to Saigon. As the bus careened down the road, Nguyen realized even though she had a little money with her, she didn't have her identity card. Like everyone in South Vietnam, when she had turned fifteen she had begun carrying a small laminated card with her name, birth date, and photo on it. Without her card, the South Vietnamese soldiers at the checkpoint would assume she was a Communist. "I was scared to death," said Nguyen. Retribution would be swift. "The soldiers just shoot you if you don't have your card."

She still didn't know what to do as they pulled up to the armed guards at the ARVN checkpoint on the edge of the city. *I have to think*, she told herself, though her

South Vietnamese civilians crowd a bus to Saigon as fighting approaches, 1975. Many took whatever possessions and supplies they could carry, including household goods, bags of rice, and bicycles.

mind was racing and spinning in fear. Everyone on the bus began filing off with their identity cards in hand, so the empty bus could be checked for weapons or stowaways. One woman who had just given birth lay where she was with her infant, too weak to get up. Seeing them gave Nguyen an idea.

She cradled baby Lai on her chest, and her mother spread a shirt over them, as if Nguyen had just given birth. Lai was so small and sick, maybe it would work.

The guard stepped onto the bus. Nguyen's heart was pounding. If he insisted she get up and go outside with the others and show her card, she'd be shot right there in front of her family. She tried to look too exhausted to even notice the guard. He walked down the aisle, shoving his gun under the seats, making sure there were no weapon caches, no Viet Cong.

The guard looked at the woman who'd just given birth, looked at Nguyen, then turned and stepped off the bus, gesturing the passengers to get back on.

Relief flooded Nguyen.

In Saigon, they made their way back to Huynh's friend's house. With the Communists so close, they were allowed to stay. They listened to the radio and the fast-moving rumors, and just hoped Huynh would find a way to get them out of Vietnam. All they knew was that the NVA moved closer to the city every day, eager to take over the capital of South Vietnam and declare victory. By April 29, the NVA had surrounded Saigon. Troops and tanks would be on the streets soon.

With only a little rice for everyone in the family to eat, Nguyen's aunt gave her a blanket and told her to sell it and buy some food. Nguyen headed to the market, which was just outside the city checkpoint. Even though she was in a hurry, Nguyen stopped to talk to the guard. She made sure he would recognize her, so he wouldn't ask for her identity card on the way back in.

The market was complete chaos. Shoppers rushed by or talked in worried clusters. Word passed from one person to another: the airport was being shelled by the NVA. Americans were evacuating by helicopter out to the waiting American ships.

Nguyen was desperate to find something for her family to eat. Finally, a woman bought her blanket, and she had enough money to get two small pieces of chicken.

As she got close to the checkpoint, she saw the guard closing the gate early, long before the curfew. She yelled and sprinted toward him. He held the gate open just wide enough for her to slip through, then pulled it shut behind her.

She ran through the city, wondering what was going on. Why had they closed the gate early? When she got back to Huynh's friend's house, everyone was gone. She realized they must be down by the water and ran to the harbor. It was in complete turmoil. Fishing boats, small river craft, and American barges crowded the shallow waters. Thousands of frantic people were trying to get onto a boat, any boat. Nguyen pushed her way through the crowd, looking for her family. Had they left without her? Was she stranded alone in a city about to fall into enemy hands? She passed barge after barge from the US Navy, all packed with refugees. Where was her family?

Miraculously, she found her mother and siblings standing at the water's edge, waiting for her. Huynh's family was on the nearest barge, moored to the pier. Nguyen's exhausted, dazed mother told her they should just go back to Da Nang.

She refused to listen to her mother. It was far too dangerous, even impossible to go back. They had to stay with her uncle's family. The barge had finished loading, but Nguyen pushed her family on board. No one stopped them.

They waited all day under the hot, hot sun without anything to eat or drink. Nobody dared to get off the barge, even for water. Finally, at ten o'clock at night, the barge moved out to sea, the swells getting larger and larger. Seasick and bone-weary, Nguyen threw up and passed out again.

When she came to, they were maneuvering alongside a much larger barge. To her, it looked like an enormous black wall against the starry sky. A cargo net was draped over its side for people to climb up.

There was no moonlight, and no time to wait for dawn. They had to load, now.

In the weak starlight, as their small barge moved back and forth on the rising ocean swells, they'd have to leap for the cargo net. Nguyen could not believe how dark it was, how tall the side of the big barge was. She watched in fear as people leaped and scrambled up the net. Finally, it was her family's turn. Her aunt and uncle jumped onto the net. She got a good grip on each kid and thrust them at her aunt and uncle one by one. They grabbed an arm or leg—whatever they could get hold of. After helping her mother, Nguyen leaped onto the net and climbed up.

The barge held several thousand refugees. As they headed away, she stared back at the coastline. She could see dozens of fires burning in Saigon, orange glows against the dark sky.

The next day, April 30, word spread through the barge: the president of South Vietnam had ordered his troops to lay down their arms. South Vietnam had officially surrendered. Far out at sea, the refugees were transferred to an enormous, multi-storied American cargo ship.

Would they go all the way to America in this ship? Would they be taken to a refugee camp somewhere, maybe in a different country? No one had any idea. It was a crushing day for Nguyen: they were alive, but torn from the other half of her family, and from their homeland.

A Vietnamese refugee climbs up a cargo net to the deck of the American ship USS White Plains, *1979. Refugees known as "boat people" continued to leave Vietnam for more than a decade after the Communist takeover, particularly during the late '70s.*

AMERICA: VETERAN

JAN SCRUGGS
APRIL 1975—MARCH 1979

"The bitterness I feel when I remember carrying the lifeless bodies of close friends through the mire of Vietnam will probably never subside. I still wonder if anything can be found to bring any purpose to all the suffering and death."

JAN SCRUGGS SLUMPED in his living-room chair watching the evening news in numb disbelief. The North Vietnamese had captured Saigon. Helicopters had pulled the last Americans off the rooftop of the US embassy while thousands of Vietnamese had filled its courtyard, trying to reach the embassy roof, some clinging perilously to the sides of the building.

North Vietnam was victorious.

It had been five years since Scruggs had served as a mortarman in Vietnam, but he felt an immediate, gut-wrenching fear for the South Vietnamese soldiers he'd fought alongside. What would happen to them? Their families? Would they all be killed by the Communists?

Vietnamese scale the fourteen-foot wall of the US embassy in Saigon, trying to reach evacuation helicopters as the last of the Americans depart from Vietnam, 1975.

Scruggs in his truck, 1975.

He thought of the tens of thousands of Americans who'd lost their lives. After years of fighting, suffering, and dying, what had been accomplished? *All that effort*, thought Scruggs bitterly, *and our allies were being conquered by tanks in Saigon.* The defeat made his service—and everyone else's—seem so pointless.

He'd spent the last five years trying to find some kind of meaning, not just for his service, but for his whole life. After returning from Vietnam, he'd moved to Washington, DC, and enrolled in junior college. He tried to avoid the antiwar protests that sometimes shut down the campus and paralyzed the entire city. "Everything was awful," he said. "People were too pissed and angry about the war to care about much of anything." If he let it slip that he'd served in Vietnam, criticism was sharp. "I can't imagine fighting peasants in Vietnam," one student said to him, "given everything I have learned about moral behavior over my lifetime." It was like a kick in the stomach.

Most nights, Scruggs drank heavily until he finally fell asleep, only to jerk awake, angry and agitated. The explosion in the mortar pit that had killed twelve of his buddies played out in his head again and again, grotesque and graphic. The men he couldn't help. The men no one had been able to save. His brothers.

One long, lonely night a few months after he returned, he decided it wasn't worth living. He took a revolver out of the locked box he stored it in, loaded it, put the muzzle to his head, and cocked it. "I went to the mirror to watch," he said. But when he got to the bathroom, he was shocked to see his reflection, with the gun pressed to his temple. Suddenly terrified the revolver would go off, he lowered it slowly, keeping his finger on the hammer. Once the gun was down, he carefully released the hammer. *It would be so stupid to kill myself now*, he thought, *after all I have been through.*

Scruggs dropped out of school and hitchhiked west. He ended up in the San Francisco Bay Area, living out of his backpack, going to rock concerts, sleeping in local parks. He kept his mouth shut about his military service, and as he wandered around aimlessly with his long hair and unwashed clothes, nobody asked.

One day at a supermarket in Berkeley, Scruggs impulsively decided to steal a pack of Hostess cupcakes. It wasn't that he couldn't buy them—he had fifty bucks in his wallet. He slipped the cellophane pack in his pocket and casually headed for the door. As he walked out, he was grabbed from behind.

Scruggs's survival instincts from Vietnam kicked in big-time. He twisted around and blocked his assailant, breaking the man's watch. As Scruggs pulled back his fist to hit the guy right in the teeth, the man reached for the revolver at his hip and yelled, "I'm a police officer and I'm going to shoot you!"

Scruggs dropped his arms. The cop picked up his broken watch and hustled Scruggs to a private room at the back of the store. He showed Scruggs his .38 caliber snub nose, and told him he'd almost put a bullet into Scruggs's chest. "You're lucky," the cop said.

"Yeah," said Scruggs, "lucky, and stupid too."

The cop told him he was going to book him. "But if I go to jail," Scruggs said thoughtfully, "I won't be able to reimburse you for your watch." He mentioned the fifty bucks in his wallet. The cop took his cash and let him go.

Scruggs didn't know why he tried to steal the cupcakes. *I had the money*, he thought in confusion. *And I'm not a thief by nature. I was raised very Christian.* All he knew was that he wasn't making good decisions since getting back from Vietnam, and this one almost got him shot. First his own revolver, and now a cop's. He had to find a way to pull himself together, to find meaning in life again.

One night at a small concert headlined by Iron Butterfly, Scruggs was drawn to one of the other performers, Country Joe. Late in the evening, Scruggs struck up a conversation with him. They ended up hanging out together for hours, listening to music and talking. Scruggs felt an immediate bond with Country Joe. He moved comfortably among both veterans and antiwar protestors, and made a distinction that eluded most protestors: don't hate the guys who served, hate the war. Somehow, being with Country Joe helped Scruggs piece together the parts of himself that felt so fractured.

In the fall, Scruggs headed back to Washington, DC, and enrolled in school again. He took classes in psychology and philosophy, searching for answers to his complicated, haunted feelings about himself and the war. He avidly read books by Robert Lifton, a psychiatrist who worked with trauma patients, including Vietnam veterans. Lifton found that many vets, like Scruggs, believed when your country asked you to serve, you had a patriotic obligation to join the military. The men often thought that fighting in the war would somehow be a testing ground of their manhood. But when they experienced others' violent deaths—both American and Vietnamese—their belief system shattered.

That fit for Scruggs.

He kept mulling over what he'd learned, and slowly life got better, especially when he met an art-school student, Rebecca Fishman. She had protested against the war, but didn't run when he told her he'd served in Vietnam.

Scruggs went on to graduate school and put together a questionnaire for Vietnam veterans about their war experiences and their return home. He found that the

Country Joe, 1971. After his electrifying performance at Woodstock, Country Joe was in demand at anti-war demonstrations and rallies, but he still loved playing small venues.

men couldn't forget their in-country years, and that the experience had isolated them from their friends, their family, and even from whom they'd been before going to Vietnam. They were often full of messy feelings, having trouble with relationships, trouble keeping a job, trouble staying out of trouble with the law.

"I understood it," said Scruggs. "It was called shell shock and combat fatigue and startle reaction." It would soon be known as post-traumatic stress disorder (PTSD).

The US Department of Veterans Affairs was slow to aid the veterans who had come back with emotional problems. Those who did try to get help felt they were being told to "get a grip." After a few frustrating attempts to get help for mental and physical problems, they often walked away, convinced the government didn't care.

By 1977, Scruggs had written articles for *The Washington Post* and *Military Medicine* exposing the maladjustment of veterans who'd seen heavy combat. He was asked to testify before Congress about veterans' struggles. To Scruggs's intense disappointment, the hearings didn't result in any significant changes in the VA's care.

Scruggs finished his degree and moved on with his life. He and Rebecca married and he took a low-pressure job at the Department of Labor in Washington, DC. He hoped the nightmares that still plagued him would eventually fade away.

Scruggs and Rebecca Fishman at their wedding, 1974.

In March 1979, he and Rebecca went to see a movie, *The Deer Hunter*, about three blue-collar guys from Pennsylvania who serve in the Vietnam War together. By the end of the violent, bloody film, one man was dead and the other two were emotionally destroyed.

Scruggs didn't go to bed with Rebecca that night, but stayed up alone. He sat at the kitchen table, gulping down glasses of whiskey. Vivid flashbacks of the battles he'd been in and the mortar explosion at the base crowded his mind. Men who'd been working together, now a tangle of body parts and broken pieces. Billy Moore, John Kroeger, John Pies, all dead.

Who would remember and honor them? *The names*, Scruggs thought as he sat alone in the kitchen. *No one remembers their names*. What about *all* the Americans who'd served and died in Vietnam? Who would remember and honor them? *They didn't just die in a car accident or some tragedy*, Scruggs thought. *They did what the government, the Congress, and the president said had to be done. They did what others didn't want to do. They were trained and went overseas and knew they might not come back. And when they don't come back, the nation owes them something.*

In the morning, Scruggs woke up with a terrible hangover, but on fire with an idea. He told Rebecca he was going to build a national memorial engraved with the names of all the American casualties of the war right in the center of Washington, DC.

It was a wild, grandiose plan. He wanted the memorial to be a place of remembrance, mourning, and celebration. The dead would have their names etched in granite, forever. The vets who'd come back struggling with their own anger, sorrow, and guilt would have a place to honor their fallen brothers. His memorial would even provide a place for reconciliation for the whole divided country.

He went straight to his boss, told him about his idea, and said he'd need a couple of days off. His boss looked him over carefully. "You know, Scruggs," he said, "we all need a mental-health day from time to time. But why don't you take a week."

Maya Lin, designer of the Vietnam Veterans Memorial, visits the construction site, 1982.

AMERICA:
MEMORIAL DESIGNER

MAYA LIN
OCTOBER 1980–JULY 1982

"I wanted my design to work with the land, to make something with the site, not to fight it or dominate it."

IN THE FALL OF 1980, Maya Lin was a senior at Yale University, taking a class on funereal architecture, studying how cemeteries and monuments reflect attitudes toward death. Someone in the class saw a flyer announcing a national competition to design a Vietnam veterans' memorial. The designs were due on March 31, 1981, long after the semester ended. But the students decided they'd like to adopt the idea for their final project, due in December. The professor agreed it would be a good, contemporary end to their studies.

In Washington, DC, Jan Scruggs had been working tirelessly for eighteen months to make his dream of a memorial into a reality. He'd paired up with two other veterans, both former military officers who had extensive political and military connections. They had opened a small office and incorporated as a nonprofit organization, the Vietnam Veterans Memorial Fund (VVMF).

The three men spoke at veterans' groups, mobilizing the dispirited veterans' community. Eager volunteers sprang into gear, getting the word out about the memorial and raising money. The VVMF lobbied members of Congress and received approval to put the memorial right on the grassy National Mall near the Lincoln Memorial, just a short walk from the White House and Congress. Scruggs couldn't imagine a more perfect place. "The idea of having all these names permanently displayed in Washington a few blocks from the White House, a block from the State Department, down the street from the US Congress—to me, this was poetic justice," he said. "These were the people everyone wanted to forget. They wanted this whole thing to go away, and I didn't want it to go away."

Once the VVMF decided to hold a competition to design the memorial, four simple guidelines fell into place: (1) The memorial needed to be contemplative, (2) It needed to harmonize with the surroundings, (3) It must contain the names of those who had died in the conflict or were still missing, and (4) It could make no political statement about the war.

In class, Lin carefully went over the guidelines and began studying war memorials for inspiration. She was drawn to World War I memorials, which often listed the names of those killed in action. "They captured emotionally what I felt memorials should be," she said. "Honest about the reality of war, about the loss of life in war, and about remembering those who served and especially those who died."

Lin felt challenged by the requirement that the memorial be harmonious to the site. She needed to know firsthand what the location looked and felt like. In late November, with only a few weeks to go before the design was due to her professor, she and two classmates drove down to Washington, DC.

The day was sunny and cool, and people were biking, relaxing on benches under the giant American elm trees, and playing Frisbee on the lawn of the National Mall. Lin walked around quietly. She started to imagine: What is war? What is death? She had a sudden impulse to make a cut into the earth, just take a knife and slice open the grassy surface, echoing the violence of war. She imagined polishing the dark earth until it was like a geode: shiny, black, and reflective. In the dark surface you would be able to see into infinity—the living on one side, the dead on the other. They'd be as close as they could be, yet unable to cross into one another's worlds. The ground, like a wound, would heal over in time.

Lin holds up a model of her winning design at the press conference with Jan Scruggs (left) *and Robert Doubek* (right), *one of the co-founders of the VVMF, 1981.*

When she presented her design for her final class project, the professor didn't think much of her concept and gave her a B. But Lin believed in her design. In the spring she quietly entered it in the national competition. She didn't yet have the drafting skills to make an architectural drawing, but instead submitted simple sketches and pastel drawings, along with a written description.

Her entry was one of more than 1,400 that poured in. The VVMF arranged to use an empty airplane hangar at Andrews Air Force Base to display them for the committee that would judge the submissions. To ensure a fair competition, each entry was given a number, and the applicant's name was sealed in an envelope taped on the back of their design. Lin's number was 1026.

Scruggs and the other VVMF members sat in a circle on folding chairs while the committee brought out the winning entry from behind a curtain. Scruggs stared in shock at number 1026's design. Their entire effort for the last year and a half had come to *this?* The biggest pastel on the board looked like a large black bat to Scruggs.

There was absolute silence as the VVMF members looked at the presentation board. The committee scrambled to explain. All the names would be listed on the two huge wings of the wall, etched into black granite.

Scruggs rose from his chair. He was thinking: *It's weird and I wish I knew what the hell it is*. He walked slowly to the front. What if the design committee had made a terrible choice?

But there was no turning back now. "I really like it," Scruggs lied. "It's a great memorial."

The members of the VVMF were in for another shock when the envelope was opened. The winner was a twenty-one-year-old college student named Maya Lin. Who was this young student with no experience, who'd beat out all the other entrants?

A few days later, Lin flew to Washington, DC, for a press conference to announce the winning design. The veterans learned she had been raised in the small town of Athens, Ohio, where her parents, both Chinese immigrants, were on the faculty at Ohio University. Lin was now in her final semester at Yale, studying architecture.

At the press conference, reporters scribbled notes, and photographers' cameras clicked as Lin went over her design. The walls would each be over two hundred feet long, and come together at a slight angle. Visitors would see themselves reflected in the dark surface, with sky and trees above.

The names, she explained, could not be listed alphabetically. There were too many men with the same last name, and they would be grouped together, which would lose their individuality. Imagine how many Joneses there would be, and Smiths. Instead, everyone would be listed by date of casualty, forever enshrined with the names of their buddies who were also mortally wounded that day.

Afterward a reporter asked Lin, "Don't you think it's ironic that the memorial's the Vietnam Memorial and you're of Asian descent?"

It hadn't even occurred to her. "That's irrelevant," replied Lin. "This is America."

During the hot, muggy Washington, DC, summer, Lin worked with an architectural firm on practical aspects of the memorial. They had to work out details like the specific placement of the memorial, the exact length needed to fit everyone's names, and the thickness of the granite.

But all summer, outraged phone calls and letters flooded the VVMF from

Vietnam vets: Why had they let a "gook" design the memorial? After all, that's who they'd been fighting. Her design was attacked as too simplistic and Asian, too modern. What was the matter with a good old-fashioned memorial?

The VVMF did their best to shield Lin from the outpouring of negativity, but communication began to break down quickly. The veterans had expected a big, prestigious design firm or architecture firm to win the contest, one headed by an experienced male. Lin was small, with long hair that fell down to her waist. She often wore baggy secondhand clothes and a big hat that made her feel safe in this strange, alien environment.

Lin felt condescended to, that they treated her like a child. It was culture shock for both sides, and the best they could do was form an uneasy alliance. As soon as her work was done in the late summer, Lin left Washington, DC. The whole process had been so difficult, she wondered: *If it had not been an anonymous entry 1026 but rather an entry by Maya Lin, would I have been selected?*

The veterans continued to work at a furious pace to raise more funds and shepherd the project through the governmental agencies that still had to approve the design.

But in October 1981, an unexpected attack came. A Vietnam vet railed against the choice of black granite. "By this will we be remembered," he wrote in *The New York Times*, "a black gash of shame and sorrow, hacked into the national visage that is the Mall." He called the design antiheroic, a trench. He was ceaseless in voicing his disapproval. "One needs no artistic education to see this memorial for what it is, a black scar," he testified at a meeting. "Black, the universal color of sorrow and shame and degradation in all races, all societies worldwide. . . . I will not stand idly by while we are memorialized by a black shaft of shame thrust into the earth."

Other vets agreed. They wanted white granite to match the Lincoln and Washington monuments. Lin stood her ground. She was adamantly opposed to changing the granite. The dark, reflective surface was a crucial part of the concept. She'd won the competition fair and square, and she still believed in her design 100 percent. She rejected the idea of any changes.

A more serious blow came at the end of December. A conservative Republican congressman asked the secretary of the interior, James Watt, to withhold approval for the memorial. It was devastating news for the VVMF.

Scruggs knew he'd lose if he engaged in a full-on fight with the congressman. Instead, he went to the press, vulnerable and undefended. "What all this goes to prove," he said, "is that this country is not recovered from the war. When people start ganging up on a guy who's just trying to honor Vietnam veterans, I think it's a lot more than aesthetics. It shows we need to do a lot more healing."

As secretary of the interior, Watt had authority over the National Mall and could stop the whole project. On January 4, 1982, he did, officially putting the memorial on hold until further notice. "Further notice" could easily be never if the arguing sides didn't come up with a compromise.

At the end of the month, the VVMF asked a sympathetic senator to arrange a private meeting between opponents and supporters so they could work out a solution. The day of the meeting, nearly one hundred people squeezed into the Senate Committee on Veterans Affairs hearing room. Veterans stood and reiterated their objections to the "black gash of shame." Finally one of the highest-ranking black officers in the American military, Brigadier General George Price, spoke. "I remind all of you of Martin Luther King, who fought for justice for all Americans," Price said. "Black is not a color of shame. I am tired of hearing it called such by you. Color meant nothing on the battlefields of Korea and Vietnam. We are all equal in combat. Color should mean nothing now."

No one dared challenge the color of the granite again, but arguing went on for hours. Finally when everyone was exhausted, a retired army general suggested the VVMF add a statue and American flag to the memorial to symbolize patriotism and the valor of the men who fought. Worn down, aware this compromise was their only chance, the VVMF agreed. The placement would be decided later.

Lin had not been invited to the meeting. When she heard about the flag and statue she was angry, and only accepted them with deep reluctance. For the first time, she felt she had abandoned her principles, and sold out.

In March, Watt issued a construction permit, and a few weeks later, bulldozers, cranes, and cement mixers swarmed the site. Crews drove concrete pilings deep in the ground to support the wall. In Tennessee, names were etched into panels of black granite imported from India. Finally, in July, a finished panel was trucked up from Tennessee and carefully put in place. The first 665 names of casualties were now on the National Mall.

Construction workers carefully guide a panel of the Wall into place, 1982. The worker gestures downward with his thumb to signal the crane operator to continue slowly lowering the granite panel.

A lone soldier overcome at the Wall during the dedication weekend, 1982.

AMERICA:
THE NATIONAL SALUTE
TO VIETNAM VETERANS

THE VETERANS
NOVEMBER 10–14, 1982

"I think it's going to be a very emotional time for Vietnam veterans. We've been freeze-dried now for a long time. This is the big welcome home we've all wanted."

SCRUGGS WAS DETERMINED to throw the best celebration the veterans could imagine. The National Salute to Vietnam Veterans would be a five-day event, Wednesday through Sunday, November 10 through 14, 1982. Scruggs had carefully timed it to include Veterans Day, observed annually on November 11. The VVMF office was crowded with volunteers organizing parties, ceremonies, speeches, workshops, concerts, a vigil at the National Cathedral, and even a parade. The highlight would take place on Saturday with the dedication of the memorial, now widely known as "the Wall."

On November 10, after frantic months of preparation, Scruggs slipped into the candle-lit chapel at the National Cathedral. Volunteers were reading the names of deceased Vietnam veterans in alphabetical order. Every fifteen minutes the readers paused for a short prayer: Catholic, Jewish, Unitarian, or Protestant. Scruggs felt a palpable sense of expectation as family members waited in the hallowed hall, then wept openly to hear the names of their loved ones spoken aloud, honored in "America's Church."

The respectful hush of the chapel was Scruggs's last quiet moment until Sunday. Out on the city streets of Washington, DC, Vietnam veterans were arriving by car, bus, plane, and even on foot. They had been waiting for this ceremony for a long, long time.

A group of veterans in Minnesota had chartered a bus to drive them to DC. One veteran on board was Gilbert de la O. It had been sixteen tough years since he'd returned from Vietnam in 1966, and he wasn't going to miss the dedication for anything. De la O was surprised there was a bar on the bus, and the driver was all for the vets having a good time. "Listen," he said, "as long as you guys don't break anything. Drink, smoke—whatever you guys want to do, I'll get you there."

De la O and the other veterans swapped stories, recalled dead buddies, and told more stories. They talked about hard times, and broke down. They'd made it back. So many hadn't. They were with other guys who understood. There was a place waiting for them in the capital, a memorial where they could stand tall and be acknowledged for what they'd been through, what they'd done for their country.

Besides celebrating, de la O had a serious mission. He wanted to honor the medic he'd served with in Vietnam. "One purpose was to go see Jimmy," said de la O, "see Jimmy Stamey's name on the memorial." Finding his buddy's name would be a chance to be with Stamey again in spirit, and to mourn his untimely death.

Lily Lee Adams flew in on a flight from Hawaii. She'd left Vietnam in 1970, but Vietnam had never left her. She came with several other women who had also been nurses in Vietnam. It was late at night when they arrived, but they headed right over to the memorial.

Groups of vets stood in clusters or sat in circles on the grass, talking quietly. Adams couldn't believe how beautiful it all was: the Wall, the vets, the peaceful feeling.

Members of various delegations of veterans gather near the Wall before heading to the memorial for its dedication, 1982.

Four veterans emerged from the crowd, stood in front of the Wall, and sang the Crosby, Stills, Nash & Young song "Find the Cost of Freedom." The song was both a remembrance and a prayer as the men's voices floated out over the audience. "They did it a cappella," Adams said. "It was about being buried underground." Everyone fell quiet, listening, lost in their own thoughts. What *was* the cost of freedom, when it was your brothers buried in the ground, swallowed by Mother Earth?

Adams walked up to the Wall, overwhelmed by the names. She wanted to find Captain Denny, the helicopter pilot who'd befriended her when she'd first arrived in Vietnam, overwhelmed and scared. She touched the granite, trailed her fingertips over a few names, then a few more. So many, many names. Which of these men had she cared for? Then, inexplicably, she was running alongside the Wall, crying, names rushing and blurring and bumping under her outstretched hand. "I wanted to be in touch with all of them," she said, "whether I took care of them or not."

For the next two days, Washington, DC, hummed with workshops, speeches, and ceremonies. Friday evening rolled around with parties and free concerts. Vets packed lounges and bars, drinking, swapping stories, searching for men they'd served with. At the Capitol Hilton hotel, a rock band turned up the volume on their amplifiers, making the walls and tables vibrate. Between songs the disc jockey kept shouting to the vets that they were heroes. The vets roared back in approval.

It rained during the night and into the early hours of Saturday morning, leaving behind wet grass and sharp, gusty winds. The vets were not about to be stopped by a little bad weather. It was time for the parade.

Fifteen thousand veterans made their way up Constitution Avenue toward the Wall. Some marched in formation, easily falling back into old cadences. Others refused. Some walked on prosthetic legs, others needed canes or crutches. Flags snapped in the bitterly cold wind, and military bands marched and played. After three hours, all the marchers had made it to the memorial, joining a crush of 150,000 people.

Speeches and prayers at the dedication were kept short. Maya Lin watched from a spot next to the Wall where she could see both the speakers and the audience. The intensity of the veterans' reactions took her breath away. She had tears in her eyes as she watched the veterans welcoming themselves home.

The crowd packs in tightly at the Wall dedication, 1982.

At three o'clock, Scruggs stood before the eager crowd and spoke of the valor of the men listed on the Wall, and the need to honor and remember them. The crowd sang "God Bless America" and the military band played. Scruggs asked for a moment of silence, then announced, "Ladies and gentlemen, the Vietnam Veterans Memorial is now dedicated."

With a loud cheer, people surged forward to touch the names on the Wall. Directory of Names books listing the location of everyone on the memorial passed hand to hand. Fingers ran down the pages, locating the panel and line number of beloved sons, fallen buddies, fathers who never came home.

De la O found Stamey's name on the Wall, Panel 12E, Row 106, and stood in the thin sunlight, memories washing through him. Before he left, he put a photo of Stamey at the bottom of the panel.

Adams located Captain Jerry Denny's name on Panel 14W, Row 83, and whispered a long, heartfelt prayer for him and his family. Unable to tear herself away, she stood next to the Wall watching people leave tributes and mementos. "There were widows who were leaving letters," Adams said. "Guys were leaving cigarettes, alcohol. And sometimes they'd write letters; this pint is for you, I was thinking about you." Visitors tucked teddy bears and dog tags at the foot of the Wall. They left muddy combat boots, flowers, flags, and Purple Hearts.

As daylight faded, veterans and visitors lingered by the Wall, touching names one last time, offering prayers and promises to return.

The Salute concluded Sunday morning where it had begun, at the National Cathedral. Scruggs read briefly from the Book of Daniel, then sat in the front row and listened quietly to the service. The celebration had far surpassed his expectations. There had been sorrow and loss, relief, reverence, and pure joy. From the very first, there had been a feeling in the air for the vets, their families, and friends: *we're all in this together.*

Welcome home, veterans. Welcome home.

Searching for a name, 1982. When combat injuries resulted in death months or years later, service members' names were added to the Wall. By 2017, 58,318 names were listed.

EPILOGUE

MORE THAN FOUR decades have passed since the United States was defeated in Vietnam, yet the veterans I interviewed had vivid memories of their year "in country." Sitting with me or talking on the phone recounting their experiences, they were flooded with turbulent, often contradictory feelings of fear, anger, sorrow, regret, and pride.

Serving in Vietnam profoundly changed all of them. "What we are talking about really is the loss of your innocence," said medic Tom Kelley. "It totally changed my life. Not necessarily for the better, but I wouldn't give it up for anything. It made me who I am." I am in awe of the veterans' persistence and inner strength as they slowly found meaningful work and fulfilling relationships with spouses and children, other veterans, and friends.

While I was weaving the veterans' personal stories into the complex, divisive web of politics and protests in America, more than a million refugees poured into Europe from Middle Eastern and African countries. It was a sharp reminder there can never be a war without refugees. Noncombatants are always caught in the cross fire: killed, injured, or on the run for their lives. I realized this book would not be complete without a civilian's story and asked Hoa thi Nguyen to share her harrowing trip to safety.

All the veterans I spoke with, no matter how they felt about serving, were acutely aware of the Wall. Kelley put off visiting for a long time, then finally went to Washington, DC. Late at night, he walked apprehensively up to the memorial. As soon as

"The Three Soldiers," designed by Fredrick Hart and dedicated on Veterans Day, 1984, stands a short distance from the entry to the Wall. The bronze soldiers (one mostly hidden here) appear to stare across the grass at the names on the memorial.

LEFT: *In 2011 Gilbert de la O found Jimmy Stamey's brother and sister, who were still living near the family's hometown of Saraland, Alabama. "I wanted to go down and see where Jimmy was buried," de la O said. "They took me over to the cemetery. That was kind of tough. But the family was just so pleased that someone was still thinking about him."*

RIGHT: *Four years after getting back from Vietnam, Henry Allen found a job with the Selma Fire Department. The work was especially meaningful to him: as a firefighter, he was saving lives and property, not killing and destroying. By 1995 he was Fire Chief, as seen here. In 2000, he went to the Wall and found the name of his childhood friend, Louis Taylor, on Panel 43E, Row 36.*

he was near, he crumpled to his knees, crying. "It was cathartic," he told me. "All those names and the black surface. It's like looking in a mountain pond at night, but with the names floating on it."

Henry Allen and Mike Horan went to honor their childhood friends who had died in Vietnam. On the eve of the tenth anniversary of the Wall, a reporter asked Scruggs to point out the names of the twelve men whose deaths had inspired him to build the memorial. Scruggs was startled. He'd never looked for them. He and the reporter walked over to panel 14W. There on rows 52–56 were the names of the men who'd been killed in the mortar explosion. Scruggs reached out and touched the carved letters. "John Pies," he read and paused, his voice cracking. "Gonzales, Gaither," he said slowly. "Kroger, Billy Moore." He wanted to honor them all, but couldn't go on saying their names. "It was just . . . I couldn't do it," he said later.

Only one of the veterans I interviewed, David Oshiro, has never been to the Wall, paradoxically because the memorial's design is so powerful. "It symbolizes every-thing Vietnam was," he told me. "To most people it's names. Dead people. But I always picture just eyes, eyes, eyes. I can't go to Washington and face that Wall. I can't have sixty thousand pairs of eyes staring at me."

When I visited the Vietnam memorial several years ago and began my quest to find and speak with veterans, I quickly realized I knew very little about the war and the politics surrounding it. I found nearly three million Americans had served "in country," almost 10 percent of their generation. Around a million Americans saw combat or were frequently exposed to enemy fire. These men and women have given us an understanding of the mental and physical suffering combat can cause, and PTSD is now acknowledged as a serious medical problem that can persist for decades.

A 2014 study by the US Department of Veterans Affairs (VA) found that veterans are 21 percent more likely to commit suicide than their civilian peers. In response to their findings, the VA set up the Veterans Crisis Line, 1-800-273-TALK (8255), staffed twenty-four hours a day. Jan Scruggs, once a trigger-finger away from suicide himself, knows how easily desperation can overwhelm vets. "If no one is there to lis-ten to them," he told me, "a tragic death can result."

The line is available to any service member, any veteran, at any time.

I began this book naively believing the Vietnam War had ended in 1975. Now I know that for those who were there, especially those with intense exposure to the war zone, the experience never truly stops for them. It will be with them for the rest of their lives. I'm deeply grateful to the eight men and women I interviewed for their courage in recounting and reliving their experiences, and letting me share them in this book.

WHAT BECAME OF THE MEN AND WOMEN
INTERVIEWED FOR *BOOTS ON THE GROUND?*

MIKE HORAN followed through on his promise to himself to go to college, and earned a bachelor's degree, a master's degree, and finally a PhD in higher education. Now retired, he worked both as an administrator and a counselor for at-risk boys. An avid skydiver, Horan has made more than three thousand jumps and serves on the board of the International Skydiving Museum and Hall of Fame. He is married and has a daughter and grandchildren.

GILBERT DE LA O went back to Saint Paul, Minnesota, and enrolled in Chicano Studies at the University of Minnesota, earning a bachelor's degree. For thirty-five years he worked with teenagers at a community center, the Neighborhood House. Saint Paul has a large population of Southeast Asian refugees, and de la O mentored Hmong teens from Vietnam. He was given an honorary Hmong name, Xia Xiong, meaning he has a strong heart. He has been married for fifty years, and has children, grandchildren, and great-grandchildren.

HENRY ALLEN returned to Selma, Alabama, and went through a difficult "trial of faith" as he struggled to become a civilian again. Repeatedly facing racial discrimination after serving his country made it all the more painful. He kept his army Bible close, and read it every day. He went on to become the first African American to join Selma's fire department and rose through the ranks to become Fire Chief. He retired in 2009 after thirty-seven years. Allen also served in the National Guard for twenty-four years. He has children, grandchildren, and great-grandchildren and volunteers at the Selma Interpretive Center and in local schools.

TOM KELLEY rambled around the United States taking all kinds of jobs, the more dangerous the better. Bizarre nightmares finally drove him to the VA for help. Realizing medics faced particular challenges, he started a support group just for medics. He now dreams only of things that actually happened, but says, "If you wake me up in the middle of the night, touch my foot. Do not get close to my head. And be talking to me when you approach." Kelley is married and works full-time in a lumber store.

JAN SCRUGGS served as president of the Vietnam Veterans Memorial Fund for nearly three decades. He organized celebrations to honor veterans and commemorate anniversaries of the Wall, as well as spearheading fund-raising efforts to keep the memorial in good repair. Today the Vietnam Veterans Memorial is the most visited memorial in Washington, DC, attracting three million visitors every year. Scruggs is chairman of the Selective Service System's National Appeal Board and an advisor to the Global War on Terror Memorial. He writes frequently for magazines and newspapers.

DAVID OSHIRO enrolled in art college in San Francisco and found work as a graphic artist. He married and has two children, but watching television footage of the Gulf War in 1990 threw him into a deep depression. He sought help at the VA and used therapy to cope with the depression and rage he was feeling. He is semiretired now, but does artwork nearly every day. Recently he had a chance meeting with a first-generation Vietnamese American engineer. Oshiro expected the man to hate all the American troops who'd been in Vietnam. But the man's eyes filled with tears, and he thanked Oshiro for his service. The hard knot of anger Oshiro had held onto for decades dissolved.

LILY LEE ADAMS switched from one nursing job to another when she returned from Vietnam, unable to settle down. She moved to Hawaii, where it was warm and humid, like Vietnam. When helicopters flew over her house, she would think she was in Vietnam and run outside to receive the patients that would be off-loading. She realized she needed help and contacted the VA. Being with others who'd served in Vietnam, especially nurses, was incredibly helpful to her. She became very involved with the Vietnam Veterans of America, and served on its National Board of Directors. Adams is married with children and grandchildren.

HOA THI NGUYEN and her family were taken by an American ship to the Philippines and flown to Guam, where they stayed in a tent, and then to Fort Chaffee, a military base in Arkansas. Some Americans were against resettling the 130,000 Vietnamese refugees brought to the United States, and host families or sponsors had to agree to take responsibility for the refugees before they could leave Fort Chaffee. After waiting for months, Nguyen and her uncle Huynh's families were sponsored by a church in Saint Paul, Minnesota, whose members helped them learn English and find schools, housing, and work. Nguyen's father died before she could go back to Vietnam to visit, but in 1995 she returned to see her siblings. She is married and has children and grandchildren.

ACKNOWLEDGMENTS

MY HEARTFELT THANKS to the people who shared with me their personal stories: Mike Horan, Gilbert de la O, Henry Allen, Tom Kelley, Jan Scruggs, David Oshiro, Lily Lee Adams, and Hoa thi Nguyen Pham. I wish I could have written an entire book about each of them, as they all had so many vivid memories. Recounting their stories, many of them left untouched for decades, could be difficult for them, and I am in admiration of their courage. Thanks also to Chinh Huynh, Hoa thi Nguyen Pham's cousin, who shared his memories of the family's terrifying trip from Da Nang to Saint Paul, Minnesota. I'm also grateful to Country Joe McDonald for his detailed recounting of Woodstock and his lifelong commitment to veterans.

As soon as I finished each interview, I turned the recordings over to Deborah Ivens Lewites for transcribing. She was fearless, fast, and laser-accurate. I can't even begin to express my gratitude.

Early on, I familiarized myself with veterans' stories by going to the Veterans History Project (VHP) at the American Folk Life Center of the Library of Congress. It's a great place to read transcripts and watch videos of veterans talking about their experiences. Visit them at www.loc.gov/vets. If you'd like to add to their database, students in tenth grade or above can conduct and submit their own interviews with veterans to the VHP.

Once I had my feet under me, I made several trips to Washington, DC, to go through the extraordinary holdings at the Library of Congress and the National Archives and Records Administration. At the Library of Congress, librarians brought me archival boxes full of newspaper clippings and correspondence, especially concerning the building of the Vietnam Veterans Memorial. The National Archives holds a large collection of photographs of the Vietnam War. My thanks to the librarians who trundled out carts loaded with boxes full of photographs for me to look through. And I would never have been able to spend so many days immersed in research if it hadn't been for Patrick W. Warren. He had no spare bedroom in his small flat, but bought me a sleeping bag and cleared a place on the living room floor where I spent many comfortable nights.

Special thanks to the people who helped me gather photos: Archivists Jay Blakesberg, Sheon Montgomery at Texas Tech, Maryrose Grossman at JFK Library, Theresa Hall at National Parks Service, and Pamla Eisenberg at the Nixon Library.

A number of writer friends listened to, read, and offered wise suggestions on my early work. My thanks to Susan Campbell Bartoletti, Tom Birdseye, Gennifer Choldenko, Diane Fraser, Anna Grossnickle Hines, Gary Hines, Suzanne Johnson, Marissa Moss, Emily Polsby, Sarah Hines Stephens, and Patricia Wittmann. Special thanks to Dennis Foley who read the book in draft form and clarified military information.

Because I was so fascinated by every bit of each interviewee's story, as well as the myriad details that made up presidents' and protestors' lives and decisions, this book required a strong, clear-eyed editor. I am incredibly grateful to Catherine Frank, who patiently and cheerfully went over what I'd written many times. Without her keen perception I would never have managed to weave these interviews into the narrative they deserved. Two copy editors at Viking deserve a special shout-out as well. My deep gratitude to Laura Stiers and Janet Pascal, who queried every single thing I asserted, and saved me from some truly embarrassing mistakes. Thanks also to my project-long shepherds, my publisher Ken Wright and my agent Steven Malk. Their enthusiasm for this project carried me from concept through to book. With (most of) the words in place, designer Jim Hoover took the reins on photographs and their placement. Collaborating with him was a flat-out delight. I loved seeing the book come to life through his visual process and keen design sense.

In the end, none of this would have been possible without the full-on support of my family. My husband, Tom, who has a near-perfect grasp of the complicated politics of the late 1960s and early 1970s, spent endless amounts of time discussing it with me. I could always count on my sons and their wives, Felix and Sasha, Will and Han, with their lighthearted queries ("How's the book going?") to keep me buoyed up. Enormous appreciation to Han's mother, Hoa thi Nguyen Pham, for sharing her story of being a refugee, and to Han for cultural understanding I was missing. And I'm lucky to have had help from Meg Partridge and Allyson Feeney, who were determined that I could organize all the materials I was trying to wrangle. And when I couldn't, they did.

SOURCE NOTES

THE HEART OF this book comes from "oral histories," personal narratives that provide detailed firsthand accounts. Unless otherwise noted, all quotations in the book are from in-person interviews, phone calls, and emails conducted by the author. For more detailed dates of individual interviews, please see the bibliography.

Vietnam: Military Advisor: Mike Horan

All quotations from Mike Horan are from personal interviews and email correspondence conducted by the author between February 1, 2014, and July 12, 2014.

America: President and Commander in Chief: John F. Kennedy

"This is another . . .": Kennedy, "Remarks at West Point."

"culminated three months . . .": Kennedy, "Telephone Recordings," November 1963.

"If, in spite of . . .": National Security Archive, "Outgoing Telegram."

To ensure American . . . their plans: McNamara, *In Retrospect*, 55.

"The way he . . .": Kennedy, "Telephone Recordings," November 1963.

"to bring . . . there.": Kennedy, "President Kennedy's Press Conference."

America: President and Commander in Chief: Lyndon B. Johnson

"We are not . . .": Johnson, "Remarks in Memorial Hall."

"Review of action . . .": Ellsberg, *Secrets*, 9–10.

"absolutely necessary.": McNamara, *In Retrospect*, 132.

"For all I . . .": Moyers, *Moyers on Democracy*, 302.

"take all . . . aggression.": "Our Documents— Tonkin Gulf Resolution."

"Our national honor . . .": Karnow, *Vietnam*, 375.

"like grandma's nightshirt . . .": ibid., 374.

"Tonight Americans . . .": Johnson, "Address at Johns Hopkins University."

"I'm not just . . .": Karnow, *Vietnam,* 418–19.

"They hope they . . .": Beschloss, *Reaching for Glory*, 356.

"We won't defeat . . .": Herbers, "Civil Rights and War."

"in no way . . .": Presidential Recordings Program, "Johnson Conversation with Martin Luther King."

"I can't stay . . .": ibid.

Vietnam: Boots on the Ground: Gilbert de la O

Unless otherwise noted, all quotations from Gilbert de la O are from personal interviews and email correspondence conducted by the author between November 16, 2013, and January 25, 2015.

"You're not accepted . . .": de la O, interview, Lideres Latinos Oral History Project.

"I'm going to . . .": de la O, ibid.

"It was horrible...": Haley, "Operation 'Abilene.'"

America: Protestor: Martin Luther King Jr.

"Never again will...": King and Carson, *The Autobiography of Martin Luther King, Jr.*, 335.

"The Children of...": Pepper, "'The Children of Vietnam.'"

"He's canceled two...": Branch, *At Canaan's Edge*, 587.

"if I was...": King and Carson, *The Autobiography of Martin Luther King, Jr.*, 336.

"break the...solidarity": King, "Beyond Vietnam."

"to divert the...": "Dr. King's Error," *New York Times*.

"stay in his place": "A Tragedy," *Washington Post*.

"and replaced it...": King, "The Domestic Impact of the War in America."

"The tragedy is...": *Meet the Press*, "Dr. Martin Luther King, Jr."

"If I am...": "American RadioWorks: King's Last March."

Vietnam: Machine Gunner: Henry Allen

Unless otherwise noted, all quotations from Henry Allen are from personal interviews conducted by the author between March 2, 2013, and July 23, 2014.

"When he got...": Utah Vietnam War Stories, "Larry Chadwick Interview."

America: President and Commander in Chief: Lyndon B. Johnson

"Every night when...": Karnow, *Vietnam*, 485.

"This is not...": Berman, *Lyndon Johnson's War*, xi.

"I am absolutely...": Willbanks, *The Tet Offensive*, 7.

"I hope they...": Karnow, *Vietnam*, 514.

"a few bandits...": Johnson, "The President's News Conference."

"To say that...": Brinkley, *Cronkite*, 378.

"If I've lost...": ibid, 379.

Vietnam: Medic: Tom Kelley

All quotations from Tom Kelley are from personal interviews conducted by the author between June 22, 2013, and January 27, 2015.

America: President and Commander in Chief: Lyndon B. Johnson

"The blow to...": Karnow, *Vietnam*, 562.

"I've made up...": ibid., 565.

"Tonight I...one.": Johnson, "Remarks on Decision Not to Seek Re-Election."

America: President and Commander in Chief: Richard M. Nixon

"I can assure...": Nixon, *The Memoirs of Richard Nixon*, 407.

January 1, 1968 to...: ibid., 369. These figures were later revised upward.

"If you can't...": Karnow, *Vietnam*, 577.

"I call it...": Haldeman and DiMona, *The Ends of Power*, 83.

Vietnam: Infantryman: Jan Scruggs

Unless otherwise noted, all quotes from Jan Scruggs are from personal interviews and email correspondence conducted by the author between March 17, 2014, and August 8, 2016.

"Billy Moore, his . . .": Chadwick, "At the Vietnam War Memorial with Jan Scruggs."

"I was ready . . .": Jan Craig Scruggs Collection, interview, Veterans History Project.

America: President and Commander in Chief: Richard M. Nixon

"I will not . . .": Nixon, *The Memoirs of Richard Nixon*, 400.

"It was a . . .": ibid., 380.

Nixon, "Presidential Daily Diary": March 15, 1969, 17–28.

"Gentlemen we have . . .": Nixon, *The Memoirs of Richard Nixon*, 381.

"It would be . . .": Schmitz, *Richard Nixon and the Vietnam War*, 48.

"great success": Haldeman, *The Haldeman Diaries*, 41.

Vietnam: Green Beret: David Oshiro

Unless otherwise noted, all quotations from David Oshiro are from a personal interview and correspondence conducted by the author between April 24, 2013, and November 19, 2015.

"Kill, kill . . . Chink.": Muller, "A Veteran Speaks."

America: Protest Singer: Country Joe McDonald

"There is no . . .": McDonald, personal interview with author, April 20, 2015.

"I don't . . . make": ibid.

"I was well . . .": Appy, *Patriots*, 197.

"Listen people, I . . .": Wadleigh, "Country Joe McDonald Live at Woodstock."

Country Joe McDonald, "I-Feel-Like-I'm-Fixin'-to-Die Rag."

Vietnam: Nurse: Lily Lee Adams

All quotations from Lily Lee Adams are from a personal interview and email correspondence conducted by the author between May 21, 2014, and November 29, 2016.

America: President and Commander in Chief: Richard M. Nixon

"If, when the . . .": Nixon, "Address to the Nation on the Situation in Southeast Asia."

"Don't get rattled . . .": Nixon, *The Memoirs of Richard Nixon*, 403.

"Great silent . . . that.": ibid, 409.

"drop a bombshell . . .": ibid., 448.

"go for broke": ibid., 450.

"It is not . . .": Nixon, "Address to the Nation on the Situation in Southeast Asia."

"bums.": Haldeman, *The Haldeman Diaries*, 161.

Would this tragedy. . .: Nixon, *The Memoirs of Richard Nixon*, 457.

"My child was . . .": ibid.

"They're lying on . . .": Taylor and Sesno, *Nixon: A Presidency Revealed*.

"This is treasonable . . .": Nixon, "Nixon Conversation 005-059."

"tawdry, miserable, filthy . . .": "Memoirs v. Tapes," chapter 4.

America: President and Commander in Chief: Gerald R. Ford

"We couldn't just . . .": Ford, *A Time to Heal*, 255.

"You are not…": Kennerly, "In the Room."

Vietnam: Refugee: Hoa thi Nguyen

All quotations from Hoa thi Nguyen are from personal interviews conducted by the author between February 22, 2013, and April 21, 2015.

America: Veteran: Jan Scruggs

Unless otherwise noted, all quotations from Jan Scruggs are from personal interviews and email correspondence conducted by the author between March 17, 2014, and August 8, 2016.

"The bitterness I…": Scruggs, "'We Were Young.'"

"You know, Scruggs…": Berkeley Graduate Lectures. "A Forum on the Experience of Veterans in American Society."

America: Memorial Designer: Maya Lin

"I wanted my…": Lin, *Boundaries*, chapter 4, page 11.

"The idea of…": Wills, "The Vietnam Memorial's History."

"They captured emotionally…": Lin, *Boundaries*, chapter 4, page 9.

It's weird… "I really… memorial.": Scruggs and Swerdlow, *To Heal a Nation*, 66.

"Don't you think…": Moyers, "A Conversation with Maya Lin."

If it had…: Lin, *Boundaries*, chapter 4, page 15.

"By this will…": Carhart, "Insulting Vietnam Vets."

"One needs no…": "Commission of Fine Arts Meeting."

"I will not…": ibid., 42.

"What all this…": Scruggs and Swerdlow, *To Heal a Nation*, 87.

"I remind all…": ibid., 100.

America: The National Salute to Vietnam Veterans: The Veterans

"I think it's…": Kenneth Bredemeier, "Preparations For Salute to Vietnam Vets Nearly Done."

"Listen, as… memorial.": de la O, personal interview with author, November 16, 2013.

"They did… not.": Adams, personal interview with author, May 21, 2014.

"Ladies and gentlemen…": Scruggs and Swerdlow, *To Heal a Nation*, 153.

"There were widows…": Adams, personal interview with author, May 21, 2014.

Epilogue

"What we… it.": Kelley, personal interview with author, June 22, 2013.

"John Pies… Moore.": Day to Day. "At the Vietnam War Memorial with Jan Scruggs."

"It was just…": Scruggs, personal interview with author, November 17, 2014.

"I wanted to…": de la O, personal interview with author, November 16, 2013.

"It symbolizes everything…": Oshiro, personal interview with author, April 24, 2014.

"If no one…": Scruggs, email correspondence with author, September 26, 2016.

BIBLIOGRAPHY

THE VIETNAM WAR—and the divisive politics and protests surrounding US involvement— is so complicated that there are thousands of books, films, websites, videos, oral histories, and more about it. For clarity, I've divided my sources into three sections: personal interviews for the powerful connection of individual stories; books for broad knowledge; online and other resources for a deep understanding of a particular subject, time, and place.

INTERVIEWS BY AUTHOR

ADAMS, LILY LEE. Personal interview by author, Santa Rosa, California, May 21, 2014. Email correspondence March 25, April 23, July 7, August 23, 26, September 6, November 29, 2016.

ALLEN, HENRY. Personal interview by author, Selma, Alabama, March 2, 2013. Telephone interviews June 18 and July 23, 2014.

DE LA O, GILBERT. Personal interview by author, Saint Paul, Minnesota, November 16, 2013. Email correspondence February 1, 3, April 22, May 5, 2014; January 25, 2015.

HORAN, MIKE. Telephone interview by author, Carrabelle, Florida, February 1, 2014. Email correspondence February 24, July 3, 6, 9, 12, 2014.

KELLEY, TOM. Personal interview by author, Berkeley, California, June 22, 2013; September 27, 2014; January 27, 2015.

MCDONALD, JOE. Personal interview by author, Berkeley, California, April 20, 2015.

NGUYEN, HOA THI. Personal interview by author, Minneapolis, Minnesota, February 22, 2013. Phone interview April 21, 2015.

OSHIRO, DAVID. Personal interview by author, San Rafael, California, April 24, 2013. Email correspondence May 4, 2014. Letters to author May 28, June 18, 2014; August 16, November 19, 2015. Telephone conversations July 7, 2014; September 1, 2015.

SCRUGGS, JAN. Telephone interview by author, March 17, 2014, Annapolis, Maryland. Personal interview by author, Annapolis, Maryland, November 17, 2014. Personal interview with author, San Francisco, California, December 3, 2015. Email correspondence December 6, 21, 2014; August 8, 2016.

BOOKS

Appy, Christian G. *Patriots: The Vietnam War Remembered from All Sides*. New York: Viking, 2003.

Berman, Larry. *Lyndon Johnson's War: The Road to Stalemate in Vietnam*. New York: Norton, 1989.

Beschloss, Michael R. *Reaching for Glory: Lyndon Johnson's Secret White House Tapes, 1964–1965*. New York: Simon & Schuster, 2002.

Branch, Taylor. *At Canaan's Edge: America in the King Years, 1965–68*. New York: Simon & Schuster, 2006.

Brinkley, Douglas. *Cronkite*. New York: Harper, 2012.

Ellsberg, Daniel. *Secrets: A Memoir of Vietnam and the Pentagon Papers*. New York: Penguin Books, 2003.

Ford, Gerald R. *A Time to Heal: The Autobiography of Gerald R. Ford*. New York: Harper & Row, 1979.

Haldeman, H. R., and Stephen E. Ambrose. *The Haldeman Diaries: Inside the Nixon White House*. New York: G. P. Putnam's Sons, 1994.

Haldeman, H. R., and Joseph DiMona. *The Ends of Power*. New York: Times Books, 1978.

Karnow, Stanley. *Vietnam: A History*. New York: The Viking Press, 1983.

King, Martin Luther, Jr., and Clayborne Carson. *The Autobiography of Martin Luther King, Jr.* New York: Intellectual Properties Management, Inc. in association with Warner Books, 1998.

Lin, Maya Ying. *Boundaries*. New York: Simon & Schuster, 2000.

McNamara, Robert S. *In Retrospect: The Tragedy and Lessons of Vietnam*. New York: Times Books, 1995.

Moyers, Bill. *Moyers on Democracy*. New York: Doubleday, 2008.

Nixon, Richard Milhous. *The Memoirs of Richard Nixon*. New York: Grosset & Dunlap, 1978.

Schmitz, David F. *Richard Nixon and the Vietnam War: The End of the American Century*. Vietnam: America in the War Years. Lanham, Maryland: Rowman & Littlefield, 2014.

Scruggs, Jan C., and Joel L. Swerdlow. *To Heal a Nation: The Vietnam Veterans Memorial*. New York: Perennial, 1986.

Willbanks, James H. *The Tet Offensive: A Concise History*. New York: Columbia University Press, 2007.

ONLINE AND OTHER RESOURCES

"American RadioWorks: King's Last March." Accessed September 7, 2015. http://americanradioworks. publicradio.org/features/king/transcript.html.

Berkeley Graduate Lectures. "A Forum on the Experience of Veterans in American Society." Accessed April 3, 2016. http://gradlectures.berkeley.edu/lecture/veterans/.

Bredemeier, Kenneth. "Preparations For Salute to Vietnam Vets Nearly Done." *The Washington Post*, November 9, 1982. https://www.washingtonpost.com/archive/local/1982/11/09/preparations-for-salute -to-vietnam-vets-nearly-done/ddc53a65-86a6-4935-97b4-0621df0c4184/?utm_term=.4cc93c6e7db6.

Carhart, Tom. "Insulting Vietnam Vets." *New York Times*, October 24, 1981. http://www.nytimes. com/1981/10/24/opinion/insulting-vietnam-vets.html.

Chadwick, Alex. "At the Vietnam War Memorial with Jan Scruggs." Accessed February 15, 2016. http://www.npr.org/templates/story/story.php?storyId=4669683.

"Commission of Fine Arts Meeting (Minutes, Transcript, and Statements)." October 13, 1981. Vietnam Veterans Memorial Fund Record, Box 29. Library of Congress, Washington, DC.

Day to Day. "At the Vietnam War Memorial with Jan Scruggs." Accessed August 7, 2017. http://www.npr. org/templates/story/story.php?storyId=4669683.

de la O, Gilbert. Interview, Lideres Latinos Oral History Project, Minnesota Historical Society, March 29, 2010. Accessed September 4, 2015. http://collections.mnhs.org/cms/web5/media.php?pdf=1&irn=10230174.

"Dr. King's Error," *New York Times*, April 7, 1967. http://kingencyclopedia.stanford.edu/kingweb /liberation_curriculum/pdfs/vietnameditorials.pdf.

Haley, Ronald. "Operation 'Abilene,'" The Home of Heroes. Accessed September 4, 2015. http://www.homeofheroes.com/wings/pitsenbarger.html.

Herbers, John. "Civil Rights and War; Peace Movements and Negro Groups Seen as Forming Closer Rela- tionship." Accessed September 8, 2016. http://query.nytimes.com/mem/archive-free/pdf?res=9806E0D8 1E39E632A25756C0A9619C946491D6CF.

Jan Craig Scruggs Collection (AFC/2001/001/86440), interview, conducted by Jeffrey Wiles, November 1, 2012. Veterans History Project, American Folklife Center, Library of Congress. http://memory.loc.gov /diglib/vhp/bib/loc.natlib.afc2001001.86440.

Johnson, Lyndon B. "Address at Johns Hopkins University: 'Peace Without Conquest.'" The American Presidency Project. Accessed January 6, 2017. http://www.presidency.ucsb.edu/ws/?pid=26877.

Johnson, Lyndon B. "The President's News Conference February 2, 1968." The American Presidency Project. Accessed July 18, 2016. http://www.presidency.ucsb.edu/ws/?pid=29149.

Johnson, Lyndon B. "Remarks in Memorial Hall, Akron University." The American Presidency Project. Accessed June 8, 2016. http://www.presidency.ucsb.edu/ws/index.php?pid=26635&st=&st1=.

Johnson, Lyndon B. "Remarks on Decision Not to Seek Re-Election (March 31, 1968)—Miller Center." Accessed March 29, 2017. https://millercenter.org/the-presidency/presidential-speeches/march-31-1968-remarks-decision-not-seek-re-election.

Kennedy, John F. "President Kennedy's Press Conference, 14 November 1963." John F. Kennedy Presidential Library and Museum. Accessed June 3, 2016. http://www.jfklibrary.org/Asset-Viewer/Archives/JFKWHA-238.aspx.

Kennedy, John F. "Remarks at West Point to the Graduating Class of the U.S. Military Academy, June 6, 1962." Accessed June 3, 2016. http://www.presidency.ucsb.edu/ws/?pid=8695.

Kennedy, John F. "Telephone Recordings: Dictation Belt 52.1. Dictated Memoir Entry." John F. Kennedy Presidential Library and Museum. Accessed August 26, 2015. http://www.jfklibrary.org/Asset-Viewer/Archives/JFKPOF-TPH-52-1.aspx.

Kennerly, David Hume. "In the Room—The Final Days of Vietnam." David Hume Kennerly. Accessed February 21, 2017. http://kennerly.com/blog/in-the-room-the-final-days-of-vietnam/.

King, Martin Luther Jr. "'Beyond Vietnam' Speech April 4, 1967." Accessed September 7, 2015. http://kingencyclopedia.stanford.edu/encyclopedia/documentsentry/doc_beyond_vietnam/.

King, Martin Luther Jr. "The Domestic Impact of the War in America." The Martin Luther King Jr. Center for Nonviolent Social Change. Accessed June 12, 2016. http://www.thekingcenter.org/archive/document/domestic-impact-war-america#.

"Memoirs v. Tapes: President Nixon & the December Bombings," chapter 4. Accessed September 10, 2016. https://www.nixonlibrary.gov/exhibits/decbomb/chapter-iv-audio.html.

Meet the Press. "Dr. Martin Luther King, Jr. on the Vietnam War and Racial Progress." Accessed November 21, 2015. https://archives.nbclearn.com/portal/site/k-12/browse/?cuecard=5092.

Minnesota Historical Society. "Interview with Gilbert De La O, March 29, 2010." Accessed September 4, 2015. http://collections.mnhs.org/cms/web5/media.php?pdf=1&irn=10230174.

Moyers, Bill. "A Conversation with Maya Lin." Moyers & Company. Accessed February 22, 2017. http://billmoyers.com/content/maya-lin-extended/.

Muller, Bob. "A Veteran Speaks—Against the War." Leatherneck.com. Accessed March 16, 2016. http://www.leatherneck.com/forums/showthread.php?1394-A-Veteran-Speaks-Against-the-War.

National Security Archive. "Outgoing Telegram, Department of State: Top Secret, Aug. 24, 1963." Accessed August 29, 2015. http://nsarchive.gwu.edu/NSAEBB/NSAEBB101/vn02.pdf.

Nixon, Richard M. "Address to the Nation on the Situation in Southeast Asia." The American Presidency Project. Accessed December 7, 2016. http://www.presidency.ucsb.edu/ws/?pid=2490.

Nixon, Richard M. "Nixon Conversation 005-059: Presidential Recordings Program: Miller Center." Accessed March 29, 2017. http://archive.millercenter.org/presidentialrecordings/rmn-005-059.

Nixon, Richard M. "Presidential Daily Diary Richard Nixon." Richard Nixon Presidential Library and Museum. Accessed September 23, 2015. http://www.nixonlibrary.gov/virtuallibrary/documents /dailydiary.php.

"Our Documents—Tonkin Gulf Resolution (1964), January 7, 1964." Tonkin Gulf Resolution. Accessed March 29, 2017. https://www.ourdocuments.gov/doc.php?flash=true&doc=98&page=transcript.

Presidential Recordings Program—Miller Center. "Johnson Conversation with Martin Luther King on Jul 7, 1965 (WH6507.02)." Accessed March 29, 2017. http://prde.upress.virginia.edu /conversations/4002519/notes_open.

Scruggs, Jan C. "'We Were Young. We Have Died. Remember Us.'" *Washington Post*, November 11, 1979. https://www.washingtonpost.com/archive/opinions/1979/11/11/we-were-young-we-have-died -remember-us/7261e945-4e24-4990-ab8d-082a2b776839/.

Taylor, David Coxon, and Frank Sesno. *Nixon: A Presidency Revealed*. Videorecording. A&E Television Networks: Distributed by New Video, 2007.

"A Tragedy." *Washington Post*, April 6, 1967, A20.

Utah Vietnam War Stories. "Larry Chadwick Interview, KUED Radio." Accessed September 7, 2015. http://www.kued.org/sites/default/files/larry-chadwick.pdf.

Wadleigh, Michael. "Country Joe McDonald Live at Woodstock, 1970." https://www.youtube.com /watch?v=Jk68D91hTXw.

Wills, Denise Kersten. "The Vietnam Memorial's History." *Washingtonian*, November 1, 2007. https://www.washingtonian.com/2007/11/01/the-vietnam-memorials-history/.

INDEX

Discarded American equipment in Long Binh, Vietnam, 1970.